REAL LIFE, REAL GOD

Real Life, Real God

Doreen Blanks

First Published in 2004 by
Malachi Press
Pine Croft
6 Larch Grove
Garstang PR3 1LE

British Library Cataloguing-in-Publication data
A catalogue record for this book is available from the British Library
ISBN 0-9547940-0-1

Printed and bound by Alden Press, Oxford

Page 82: quotation from *Clippings from my Notebook* by Corrie ten Boom,
published by Triangle SPCK, 1983.
Two other books acknowledged are *9 O'Clock in the Morning* by Dennis Bennet
and *Prison to Praise* by Merlin Carothers both published by
Coverdale House Publishers.

Foreword by
Rev. Dr William R. Davies M.A., B.D.

Christians are a pilgrim people and every Christian is on a pilgrimage. The terrain through which each one of us passes is varied with its mountaintops and valleys, its rough places and plains. Each Christian has his or her own story.

One reason why these stories are so important is that they are a source of inspiration and encouragement to those who read them. We can all learn from the experiences and insights of others as they share them with us.

It has been my privilege to have known Doreen and David Blanks for over thirty years and it gives me pleasure to commend Doreen's testimony.

Doreen tells things as they are. In her testimony, the ordinary is mingled with the extraordinary and she shares her sorrows as well as her joys. This is no book of theological triumphalism but one in which the problems and testing times of faith, of which Doreen has had her share, are honestly and openly recounted. It has the ring of truth and reality and should command a wide readership.

I have no doubt that as people read of Doreen's experiences and of her testimony to the love of Jesus Christ and the power of the Holy Spirit they will find blessing and encouragement for their own Christian pilgrimage. Maybe for some it will be the cause of a Christian pilgrimage begun.

William R. Davies.

Dedication

In memory of our dear son, Martin

Acknowledgements

I would like to say thank you to the Holy Spirit who gave me the project, to family and friends, fellow writers, and all who have encouraged me with it, particularly David, who has picked me up after all the rejections and has recently taken to calling it my M.O. (Magnificent Obsession).

Thank you to all who are surprised to find that they appear in the book almost by accident of time and place because they played a part on my life at one time. Apologies to those who have played a part but not got a mention.

All biblical references are taken from the New International Version of the Bible published by Hodder & Stoughton, unless otherwise stated.

CHAPTER ONE

Glimpses of childhood

God Provides

'Give and it will be given to you. A good measure, pressed down, shaken together and running over will be poured into your lap.' Luke 6 verse 8

"Come on Doreen, time to get up it's your turn to feed the ducks," said Mum, as she came bustling into my bedroom with an early morning cup of tea. I loved the ducks and the eggs they gave us but it was bad enough trying to get myself out to school without having to feed them as well! I remembered how we had got the ducks. Mum did not usually buy raffle tickets but she had bought some to support the Red Cross and won a sitting of duck eggs. A neighbour had lent her a broody hen to bring them off. We laughed as the hen tried to persuade the newly hatched ducklings that they did not wish to swim on the pond we had made for them.

Mum was right, it was Tuesday it was my turn, so instead of turning over and moaning, I sat up and drank the tea.

Mum was slim, dark and pretty with dark smudges under her eyes. To call her slim was to be polite she was distinctly skinny after the years of war and rationing. Dad had been away in the army for most of the war. Mum kept us fed eking out the meagre rations by having a kitchen garden and the ducks.

Mum's day went something like this:

After seeing Joan and me safely off to school she bustled around in the kitchen to clear the way for the mountain of ironing. The whole weeks' family wash had been laboriously done the previous day using a gas copper, sink and scrubbing board. The ironing had to be done now with two black flat irons that she heated on the kitchener. This was a black coal-fired stove which heated water, had an oven and hotplates. It was a bit like a crude type of Aga. If I used it, it had just two heats – burning hot and nearly cold! But Mum managed to produce good meals from it and delicious cakes as well.

She put the irons to heat on the stove and waited till they were hot. She picked one up with a thick oven glove and spat fiercely on to it, when steam hissed off it she knew it was ready. Carefully she tested the iron on a piece of waste material to remove any dirt and once again test the heat. The linen things were ironed first because they could stand the heat best of all, then the cotton and so on until the iron was too cool to iron anything else, then it was replaced on the stove and another tested. She turned on the wireless. "Ah good," she thought "there is still some power left in the accumulator but I'll have to send one of the girls to the garage to get it recharged." It usually fell to our lot to take it. It was quite heavy and we had to take it on a bus, being very careful not to spill any of the acid – a journey we did not enjoy.

She had barely made a start on the pile of ironing when someone knocked at the door. Carefully Mum put the iron back on the stove and went to answer it. Standing there was a neighbour holding out a collecting box for the Red Cross.

"Oh," said Mum, "Hello, Mrs Berry, how are you?"

"Fine thanks," she replied.

"And Frank and Freda?"

"Frank's still very deaf after that last doodlebug. How are you?"

"We're alright. Bill's still quite unsettled at work – that time away has taken it's toll. The girls are fine, though they're always hungry, I'm sure they must have hollow legs!" She paused and then said, "I'll just go and find my purse."

As she went back into the kitchen she knew only too well what she would find there. She had just half a crown to buy something for our dinner.

What shall I do? She thought – yet she already knew what she would do, she could never refuse to give to charity. With barely a second thought she went back to the door and put the money into the box – we can always have eggs for dinner.

She returned to the kitchen to continue the ironing thinking no more about it.

As she sat after lunch drinking a well-earned cup of tea and listening to Woman's Hour she heard a "Cooee" coming from the back door.

Mum recognizing the voice said, "Come in Min, would you like a cup of tea?"

"Yes, why not, Arthur's not coming in for one this afternoon, he's too busy on the nursery" said my Auntie Min who lived just across the road.

"I've brought you this saucepan of lamb stew, we had it for our dinner – I made too much. Arthur won't eat stew again tomorrow; you know what he's like. Wondered if you could use it up?"

Mum laughed out loud and said "We certainly could use it, I was only saying to Mrs Berry this morning that I think the girls have hollow legs! It's very kind of you " and then she related to Auntie Min the story of the half crown.

As we ate our meal that night we enjoyed it all the more as Mum told us this story, and the stew fed us for two days.

Renovations

' And my God will meet all your needs according to his glorious riches in Christ Jesus.' Philippians 4 verse 19

My childhood home was a pretty looking pebble-dashed bungalow set in a large garden behind a beech hedge. It was a pre-war prefab made of asbestos. It was cold and ran with condensation. For years we had no electricity, no bathroom and an outside chemical closet.

Bath night was Thursday, nobody went out and no visitors were allowed. Before tea Mum lit the gas copper and stoked the black kitchener stove while Joan and I carried the tin bath into the living room. After tea Mum poured the hot water into the bath while Joan and I undressed. Mum washed us all over and shampooed our hair with green soft soap, then, after a rinse, we climbed on to Mum's lap and snuggled into a warm, fluffy towel. Sometimes Mum wound rags into our damp hair so that after a night in bed we had beautiful ringlets – at least for an hour or two – instead of the usual plaits. Once dried and in our pyjamas we went to bed. Then they topped up the bath with water and it was Mum and Dad's turn.

After the war, when Dad was back home again and my second sister Ann was born, Uncle Arthur who rented us the bungalow said he would have electricity and a longed-for bathroom with a W. C. put into it.

When Mum heard about the renovations she was anxious. We had difficulty making ends meet from week to week without having to find money for lampshades and other electrical goods. So she prayed about it.

Mum was always the one in the family who had a strong faith in God. She had been brought up to go to the Methodist Church. For some time before her marriage she had attended Westminster Central Hall and I remember as a child, hearing the charismatic preacher Rev. Dr William Sangster there.

Dad belonged to the Band of Hope when he was a child – a Christian temperance movement that encouraged young people to sign the pledge not to drink alcohol – a pledge he did not keep when he grew up. As a young man his faith in God was very fragile and his time as a soldier in Egypt destroyed any vestige. He did not speak much about that time to us but he declared more than once. "When you're dead, you're dead, there's nothing else."

Dad was a keen football pools man – he didn't spend much, otherwise he would have had Mum to deal with, but he did a line or two. One Saturday around the time of the renovations we sat in silence at 5.30 p.m. as Dad listened to the football results on the wireless. The battery was running low so we did not dare to move a muscle or he'd have missed it! Mum did not really approve – "Methodist's don't gamble". Excitement grew as Dad checked his coupon, he had 23 points on one line. 24 points was what was needed for a jackpot but Dad had 23 points. Later that evening a large dividend was predicted for the winners and Dad was hopeful that he would collect a fair amount.

He won around £245, a tidy sum in the late 1940s. It paid for all the electrical goods we needed and some that we <u>wanted</u> including a wireless – what a relief, no more taking the accumulator to the garage to be recharged!

Fifty pounds of that money paid for our only holiday as a family. We went to Bournemouth, ration books in hand, for a fortnight. Mum made us beach clothes from old curtains and we had a wonderful time.

How could Mum come to terms with this windfall? – She had prayed for God to help us and the money came through a win on the football pools. In the end she accepted it gratefully and enjoyed the blessings it brought us.

First steps to Faith

'For God so loved the world that he gave his one and only Son that whoever believes in him shall not perish but have eternal life.' John 3 verse 16

As a family we observed certain Christian rituals every day. We said or sang 'Grace' before meals and Mum or Dad always heard us saying our prayers.

'*For what we are about to receive may the Lord make us truly thankful*' was the most common prelude to our tea although

Thank you for the world so sweet,
Thank you for the food we eat,
Thank you for the birds that sing,
Thank you God for everything

was another. – we sang this one.

At night Mum – or Dad, when he was there – would read us a story then listen to us as we gabbled a prayer –

"God Bless Mummy, God Bless Daddy, God Bless Joan, God Bless Ann, God Bless Aunties, Uncles, Cousins and all kind friends. Help me to be a good girl. Amen."

Then there was a kiss and a cuddle "Goodnight, God Bless" and we snuggled down into our feather beds covered with blankets and eiderdowns.

During war time evenings in double summer time it stayed light so long that we had difficulty sleeping and occasionally we would go out for a walk with Mum. Other times we pestered her with "I want a drink of water!" as she wrote her letters to Dad away in Egypt.

One particularly hot summer evening during the holidays we had Auntie Meg and our cousins Evelyn and David staying so they decided to take us all out for a walk. We three girls ran on ahead up a steep hill while David, dawdled behind. David suddenly ran up to his Mum shouting "Look Mum black gloves! Do you want black gloves too Mummy?"

Mum and Auntie Meg looked on in horror, his hands and the front of his clothes were covered in melted tar. Our walk curtailed we returned home and Mum used her precious dripping to try and remove the tar from hands and clothes.

On Sunday afternoon we were packed off to Sunday School at the local Methodist Chapel – little more than a hut with a coke burning stove to toast our feet and a harmonium to provide the music. Mrs Poynter, who played the harmonium was very tiny and could barely reach the pedals. We watched her carefully as we thought she might wobble off the stool – she never did and managed to provide us with a good tune.

Mrs Goode, the Sunday School Superintendent, an elderly, slightly stooped lady with bright twinkling eyes shining out of a kind face, was an enthusiastic teacher.

She lived up to her name.

We had Bible lessons, colouring and puzzles and sang choruses like 'I am H-A-P-P-Y', and 'I will make you fishers of men'. Each year we were encouraged to take a Scripture exam when we learnt Bible stories and a few verses – called a 'memory passage', by heart. We learnt them from the King James Version but 50 years on I still remember several of them.

One day each year 'Decision Cards' were handed round and each of us was encouraged to fill one in. They said something like this:

'I _____ ask God to forgive my sins and come and live in my heart.'

I remember filling one of these in when I was eleven and knowing that I meant it. It was the same year that I passed the eleven plus exam and went off to Grammar school.

At Grammar school I joined the Christian Union in which people of several denominations gathered to talk about their faith and discuss the Bible. From Baptist to Christadelphians joined in the discussions. The Christadelphian Miriam and I had the same birth date so we called each other 'Twinnie'. I admired her knowledge of the Bible and found that Christadelphians were expected to read through the Bible every year. This was a place where we encouraged one another and my faith began to grow until I left school at sixteen.

That same year our church arranged for a coach to take us to Harringay to hear the American evangelist Billy Graham. Some churches thought his methods were too slick and highly organised but ours was willing to give him a try.

As we went to find our seats a well trained choir sang hymns and there was a buzz of anticipation in the air. The meeting began with hymns, prayers, readings and a solo from George Beverley Shea. Then the moment came when Billy Graham stood up to speak. In that vast arena you could have heard a pin drop. He gave the Gospel message with a clarity that I had never heard before. How Jesus had died on the cross and taken our sins with him. All we had to do was to be really sorry for those sins, want to change and ask him to forgive us. Then he would come into our hearts and live within us and we would enter into eternal life.

Then came the appeal "If you would like to ask God to forgive your sins and ask Jesus to come and live in your heart I would ask you now to get up out of your seats and come down into the arena where coun-sellors are waiting to speak to you". As the people began to move we sang the very moving hymn:

Just as I am without one plea,
But that Thy blood was shed for me
And that Thou bidd'st me come to Thee,
Oh Lamb of God, I come

Soon people were coming down the aisles like lava down the sides of a volcano and I knew I had to join them in a public declaration of my love for God. From now on it was out in the open, no longer a secret between God and me.

This experience strengthened my faith and my relationship with God grew and became more real. My counsellor, a young woman, kept in touch and encouraged me for two years.

CHAPTER TWO

Growing Up

Decisions, Decisions, Decisions!

*'And we know that in all things God works for the good of
those who love him who have been called according to his
purpose.'* Romans 8 verse 28

Over the next few years I had some vital decisions to make and I prayed
about them. Guidance is something that is difficult. I wish God would
'put the writing on the wall' as he did in the book of Daniel. But He
seldom does it that way – for ordinary mortals like me.

Here I was sixteen years old with three GCE 'O' levels to my name,
what should I do next? I had no idea what job to apply for, although, at
least at that time, there were plenty of jobs available.

Brenda, a school friend said, "I'm going to work in a bank."

That sounded like a good idea – one of my GCEs was Maths – so I
said, "I think I'll do that too!" Which is how I found myself working at
Westminster Bank in the City of London, just a few weeks later.

My weekly wage was good for a sixteen year old – £4 5 shillings. From
that I had fares to pay for the ten-mile journey, a contribution at home
for my keep, lunches and clothes. I delighted in handling some of my
own money – not always wisely. I was able to select my own clothes – not
having sisters, cousins or friends cast-offs was bliss! There was a pale
turquoise woollen coat with a fur collar that I bought at a newly opened
expensive boutique – it spent most of its time at the cleaners. Then there
was a pair of red corduroy trousers that my boyfriend called 'passion
pants', which horrified Dad. There was also a blue windcheater – the
precursor to the anorak that I could only wear at weekends but I loved
it. I did have some successes too, some very pretty cotton dresses and a
lovely pale turquoise evening dress that I wore till it fell apart.

At seventeen I met the young man who would eventually become my husband. I had seen him before when he marched with the Boy's Brigade band down to our little country chapel to take part in a service. My mother noticed him and nudged me saying, "That boy [he was probably about fourteen then] has a cheeky face!" The cheeky face has changed but the cheeky attitude is still there. He is the only one of her 3 sons-in-law who got away with calling mum 'the dragon'!

We met properly at a church weekend youth conference held at High Leigh Conference Centre in Hertfordshire. The group we were with got together after the Saturday evening session and we paired off. David sought me out and we began seeing each other on a regular basis after that. I can't say that I sat down and prayed about it, I just knew I liked him and he was a Christian so that was how it started.

David was just eighteen when we started going out together. Unfortunately, soon after we met he received his call up papers to do his national service. This time was to be a great test of our relationship; we met in the February and in the June he was away in Portsmouth doing basic training with the RAOC (Royal Army Ordnance Corps)

During those first few months he took me to his church at South Chingford where there was a strong Young Peoples Fellowship group. It was good getting to know more young Christians, as we had few of my age in our little chapel at Sewardstone. They were a great encouragement to me while he was away.

We kept in touch by letter and the postman must have smiled as the letters came with H O L L A N D (Hope Our Love Lives and Never Dies), or S W A L K (Sealed With A Loving Kiss) on the back of the envelope.

The army was an eye – and ear – opener for David. He came from a Christian working class home with just one older brother. Here he had to share his life with many young men who hardly spoke without swearing and were used to a very different life.

After about six months David was posted to Greenford in Middlesex and was able to come home most weekends. During these two years we each changed a lot. We did a lot of growing up. There was a time when I thought the relationship was over but we talked things through and got back together.

I joined the Christian Union at the bank, giving me fellowship with a mixed group of people who were mostly older than me. This gave me another opportunity to grow in my faith.

As soon as he was demobbed David went back into Insurance to work. Then one day while we were out walking he asked, "Will you marry me?"

"Yes of course I will!"

Then his practical side came into the conversation "We'll have to wait a while, I want us to buy a house. We'll need to save up."

We planned together to make our engagement official on my twentieth birthday. We hoped to marry two years later, if we'd saved enough for a deposit on a house and a few sticks of furniture to put in it.

Man proposes and God disposes is sometimes used to describe how life plans can be changed by unforeseen circumstances. This happened to us. David's mother had died suddenly when he was sixteen and after her death his paternal grandmother- Nan – had moved in to look after him and Pop – David's father was always called Pop.

Nan was a rather sharply spoken woman who had a tough life. She did not suffer fools gladly and could be outspoken. One day I called and had on a smart royal blue suit (one of my latest successes). As I entered the room Nan said, "Cor you look smart for a change!"

I did not know whether to feel flattered or flattened!

We had been engaged for just over a year and the saving was going well when Nan was taken ill with cancer and died. Soon after her death Pop approached us with a proposal, he said, "How would it be if I sold you this house with it's contents and I continued to live here with you?"

We said we'd think about it.

"Seems like a good idea and it would mean we could get married sooner" said David ever practical.

"Sounds alright, I like the house and I like your Dad but it's very different actually living with someone!"

"We could get married this year if we did buy the house from Pop."

"We had my Nan living with us for a while – it was awful – loads of arguments!"

The discussion went back and forth. We were young and in love, the temptation was too great, so we accepted his offer and brought the wedding forward six months.

Two vital decisions made – decisions that would affect the rest of our lives. Pop lived with us for the next twenty-eight years. Did we make a mistake? I still wonder, but I have to think it comes under the text at the start of this chapter. *'And we know that in all things God works for the good of those who love him who have been called according to his purpose.'*

Marriage and Children

'For this reason a man will leave his father and mother and be united to his wife and the two will become one flesh.'
Matthew 19. verse 5

We planned our wedding for September 1959 with my two sisters as bridesmaids, and David's brother Cliff as best man. The Bridesmaids wore turquoise and I had a white princess style flocked nylon dress with a deep v-neck. We had real pale yellow roses in our headdresses and bouquets – mine were mixed with freesias.

We married at David's home church at South Chingford. It was a lovely service and the reception was held in the church hall with Mum supervising the catering. One thing David remembers about the reception is that the tomato soup was burnt! I remember little, the day seemed to pass in a happy blur.

After the reception people were invited to go back to our house to view the Wedding presents. One little lady,.who had been at the reception, turned up and I guess that everyone had thought she was a member of the 'other' family. She was in fact a lady from the church who had gate crashed!

We changed into our going away clothes. These were, for us, motorcycle gear, including crash helmets, as we were off to Norfolk on our 197c.c. James motorbike. As we left we passed several of the guests who looked amazed at our transformation.

Home from a beautiful sunny fortnight of honeymoon, we began living with the reality of having a parent living with us. Making love with father-in-law in the next room was a distinct passion killer.

Soon after we came back, David and I had an argument that extended over the washing up. Pop didn't say a word but the look of disapproval was enough. He did not usually venture an opinion, unless asked, but his looks spoke volumes.

We soon settled down into a routine and as we all three worked, we shared the household chores. Slowly we bought our own furniture and decorated the house to our taste. Somehow, though, it never seemed to be my home – it was David and Pop's home but never really mine. I felt like an interloper.

We continued to go to Y.P.F. and David studied to get his A.C.I.I. (Associate of the Chartered Insurance Institute) insurance examinations and became a Local Preacher at Church too. A Local Preacher in the Methodist Church is a lay man or woman who feels called to preach, but not to the ordained ministry. Methodist Churches are arranged in Circuits with perhaps two ministers to eight churches, so Local Preachers fill the pulpits of the other chapels.

Time passed quickly and after three years we decided it was time to start a family. Within two months I was pregnant. Morning sickness came twice a day for me, returning as I cooked the evening meal and it went on for months. Otherwise I kept quite well. I looked forward to the birth with mixed feelings. I knew that it was painful but reasoned that it could not be too bad as so many women had more than one child – ignorance is bliss! I also thought that the baby would fit neatly into our life and life style.

My pregnancy was over a very cold, snowy winter and it soon became obvious I needed a new winter coat that would cover the bulge. We went to the local shopping centre and the search began. In desperation we went into an upmarket shop. I looked on the rails and the first one I tried was a royal blue and black soft tweed coat, with a Persian lamb collar, that was full enough to encompass the bulge. I walked up and down the shop preening.

"How much is it?" David asked the assistant.

I can't now remember how much it was but it was above our budget. Seeing my husband's shocked face she added "But it is a genuine Worumbo, sir!"

"Is that good?" asked David with the usual twinkle in his eyes.

The assistant, a little nonplussed, smiled and said, "It really is a good coat, sir."

"It should be for that price!" he retorted.

Meanwhile knowing the price and our budget, I took off the coat and began scanning the racks once more. A plain light blue coat looked nice on the rack, but not on me. A green tweedy one fitted me now but would not allow for the expected expansion.

By this time David was getting rather restless and in desperation brought over the 'genuine Worumbo' and said, "Try this one again".

I snuggled into it and paraded up and down the shop.

"It's more than we can really afford," said David, "but it is a lovely coat which fits you well and suits you too. We'll have it," he said, turning to the assistant. "I hope this 'genuine Worumbo' will be as good as you say!"

I kept that coat for many years. It saw me through both my pregnancies in warmth and comfort. Now if ever I am shopping for a coat with David he will smile and say, "but is it a genuine Worumbo?"

The due date for the baby's birth came and went. Two days later the contractions started and David rushed me to the maternity hospital where they promptly stopped. Soon after our arrival I was examined and the doctor, whilst pummelling my stomach, muttered something that I overheard, "There seem to be too many limbs it could be twins". So off I went for an X-ray which revealed just one baby. This left me thinking that my baby had extra arms or legs until I actually saw him for myself. David was sent home once visiting time was over and soon after he had gone the contractions started again and our son Martin was born on 10 May 1963. I remember illogically thinking at the moment of the birth it's a girl, but then being told the reality a moment after.

The coming of this new baby changed our lives again forever. This wonderful little bundle was a joy – but he terrified me too. I was used to girls, now I had to learn about boys. We were entirely responsible for caring for this new life. He took us over completely. If he seemed too quiet I went in to look at him and if he seemed too still I poked him just to make sure he was still alive. He took all my time and I barely seemed to have time to feed myself or do anything else.

I did everything by the book, in those days you fed your baby every four hours whether he needed it or not. You were not encouraged to pick them up if they cried. I was determined to feed him myself, and I did till he was 7 months old, despite many problems.

One memorable day I decided I would take him to the clinic for the first time. It was open from 2–4 p.m. I fed him, changed him and put him in a smart outfit – I wanted to show him off- then I squeezed into a pre maternity outfit. I picked him up to put him in the pram and he vomited all over both of us. I changed him, and myself, and almost ran to the clinic arriving just before it closed.

He was generally a happy child though as a tiny baby he had colic in the evenings. It usually started at about the time David came home from work and his crying lasted spasmodically till about 9 p.m. He soon became a smiler. He inherited my dimples. At three months old he chuckled out loud. I might have doubted it if I had been there by myself but Pop was there and heard it too!

I had a fit of the baby blues for a few weeks after he was born and can remember standing over the sink washing nappies and crying – saying to myself, "What are you crying for you're a Christian, you have a lovely baby, husband and home you should be happy" – but hormones don't understand these things!

We were the first couple in Y. P. F. to have a baby and we did not fit in there any more. I did not know quite where I fitted into the church and I did not have time for prayer and Bible readings for months on end. We carried on going to church and I did still believe in God and prayed in my quieter – and desperate moments.

I became pregnant again. The house we had bought from Pop had just two bedrooms and a box room, now I was pregnant again we needed space for this new baby. So we started searching around London for a larger property. Both David and Pop worked in the City of London so they needed to have access to trains or underground to get them there.

We finally found a house on a new estate in Broxbourne, Hertfordshire. This was a really good move for me. This was <u>our</u> house; a house David and I chose together and we watched it being built. It had four bedrooms and as an extra we had central heating installed.

Broxbourne was a good place for fellowship in the church at Hoddesdon. We belonged to a house group for young couples and there was a lively Sunday school for the children as they grew.

This pregnancy was not without difficulty the sickness returned and then about half way through I was taken ill with Nephro-pyelitis and rushed into hospital one night. I discovered much later that I, and my baby, were fortunate to survive. When he woke next morning Martin found me gone and he did not understand what was going on. I was in hospital for a few days and my sister-in-law Joan looked after him for us. When I went home I could not wait to see him but when I arrived he ignored me totally and carried on playing with his cousins. I was heart-broken. I had destroyed his trust, which took a while to restore.

Sally was born at home in May 1965 about 6 weeks after we moved to Broxbourne. I was delighted at the prospect of having her at home. David had been excluded from Martin's birth but this time he could be there.

Sally took a long time to come – she was facing the wrong way. Mum and Dad came to be with me and look after Martin. Dad got fed up with me walking up and down the room. In desperation he said, "If you don't stop pacing up and down you'll wear a hole in the carpet!" – But I still could not stop!

Martin had been 7lb 13 oz at birth Sally was 9lb 8oz – long and thin as she is even now – she is 5 foot 11 inches tall.

I was much more relaxed with this new baby and took on board the suggestions coming from the latest 'baby experts' of feeding on demand. I tried to feed her myself but gave up after about six weeks. She thrived and slept through the night much sooner than Martin had. She too is a smiler. The children loved each other. As they grew they squabbled, but if an outsider did anything against the other they would soon come to each other's defence.

We made good friends in Broxbourne with neighbours and church people. David passed his second set of insurance exams becoming a Fellow of the Chartered Insurance Institute. The children grew and Martin started playgroup and then school. Sally started playgroup too.

This was the time when I started questioning my faith, the housegroup was a good place to question and I took the opportunity. It was not that I doubted God or my faith in Him but I questioned whether I was grow-ing spiritually as much as I should have been. I felt my character should have been improving – the fruits of the Holy Spirit of love, joy, peace, patience, kindness, goodness, gentleness and self-control (Galatians 4) – where were they in my life? Some of the promises in the Bible were not being fulfilled in my life nor in the life of the church. Jesus told his disciples to preach the Gospel and heal the sick, cast out demons and raise the dead. This was for his disciples now too but, as far as I could see, it was not happening. The key seemed to me to be in the power of the Holy Spirit. So I sought for Him.

Two things showed up my inadequacy, the first was a friend who was plagued with phobias and I thought we should be able to do something more to help her than we did. We did practical things like take her out when she could not go on her own. I was convinced that Jesus would have healed her and we were his representatives, why could we do nothing?

Then some neighbours had a car accident in which their 5-year-old son was killed. I did not know what to say to them – how could I comfort them?

We did meet a Malaysian man called Edgar who had 'something' and God used him for healing although he wasn't able to help our friend with phobias.

We had been in Broxbourne four years when David came home with some startling news. After the children had gone to bed he said, "I'm going to apply for a job in Manchester."

"I don't want to live in Manchester!"

"Hang on a minute, I haven't got the job yet!"

"It's just my luck if you do get it! I'm happy here. What's the job anyway?"

He told me that an older Local Preacher, Mr Everitt, from our previous Circuit who was also in Insurance, had contacted him saying that the Methodist Insurance Company in Manchester were looking for a new General Manager and had suggested David might apply.

David had looked into the possibility of going into the Ministry of the Methodist Church shortly before and had been told on a weekend course that they did not want insurance men in the Ministry. With the suggestion from Mr Everitt that this might be 'the finger of God,' David felt he should apply.

It was 1969 when David applied for the job and was interviewed. Although he was only 32 he was offered the post. So my worst fears were realised we had to move away from childhood home, family and friends to live near Manchester. I knew that David felt that this was a calling from God and I also knew with my head, although not in my heart at that point, that if he were right, we would be blessed in the move.

As we were moving to a part of the country that we did not know we wondered where we should live. David was used to commuting so had no intention of living in Manchester itself. Pop had retired just that year. We talked to a lady at church who had a daughter who lived in Knutsford in Cheshire and Cheshire being south of Manchester (that bit nearer to London and the family) seemed like a good place to start looking.

We went to stay for a weekend in Hale with the retiring Managing Director and his wife, and found a house on a new estate in Alderley Edge. We put down our deposit and returned to Broxbourne where our house was on the market.

David was due to take up his post in January 1970. To our horror in December we heard from the builder that we had been too slow to pay the full 10 per cent and they had sold the house to someone else. We had been trying to arrange a bridging loan, as our present house had not yet sold.

On Friday 13 December we left the children with Mum and Dad and, determined to find another house, went for the day to Cheshire. It was a long tedious journey in our elderly Ford Consul car – it was before the M1 and M6 had been joined.

Drifting fog greeted us as we entered Knutsford – we were not very impressed, but as we toured around the town Knutsford grew on us and we found a small new estate on the edge of the town. We liked one of the houses so we put a deposit on it and drove wearily back to Hertfordshire. One thing that pleased us was that we would get a better house for our money in Cheshire than in Hertfordshire.

New Life in Knutsford

'And we know that in all things God works for the good of those who love him, who have been called according to his purpose.' Romans 8 verse 28

Was it just coincidence that it was April fools day? It was April lst 1970 and I stood looking out of the hotel window surveying Knutsford Heath thinly covered with snow. Perhaps all the tales told in London about the frozen north of England were true. Today we were to move into our new home. It would be the start of a whole new life for us all, how would we cope?

I was brought back to the present with a jolt as David, practical as ever, broke into my thoughts. "Come on love, if you don't hurry the removal men will be at the house before us."

"Have we made the biggest mistake of our lives? It's such a long way from our families and friends. And look at the weather!"

"Only time will tell, let's look on it as an adventure!"

The first two or three years in Knutsford were, for all of us, a difficult time of adjustment. Martin in a new school found he was lagging behind with reading and multiplication tables.

Sally started school for the first time and settled much better than she ever had in playgroup. Each day as I took her to playgroup she would cry when I left and I went home feeling the worst mother ever. The play-group supervisor assured me that as soon as I had gone she settled down and started playing happily and suggested I stay a while and peep in the window. I did and it was true.

David found his new job interesting and challenging and set about making changes.

Pop found it difficult to settle, he was completely out of his element, he'd lived all his life in the suburbs of London and now suddenly at sixty-five he was living on the edge of the country. He'd spent his working life in a cigarette factory, which seemed quite a different life from most of the people he met now. At least he was fit and could walk the mile into Knutsford to the Library or shops. He loved to read. He too was involved in the Church but was always something of a loner. With time on his hands he helped a lot with the garden and took up oil painting. He'd done watercolours when he was at school.

We all missed my parents and our sisters and brothers and the children missed their cousins too. We used to go often for Sunday lunch at Mum's while we lived at Broxbourne, so they left a big hole in our lives. We went back often to see them. Each time we left them to come back to Knutsford the children would be in tears, and, Pop sitting in the back seat of the car, would cuddle the children to comfort them. None of us liked to leave our family, and adults too, felt near to tears. We decided that the only way we had a chance to settle was to go south less often.

The local Methodist church was very welcoming. The minister and one of the stewards came to visit us the day we moved in – we entertained them among the packing cases!

The junior church was a large one and the children soon felt at home there. I joined the Young Wives group and David carried on with his Local Preaching. There were plans afoot to demolish the old Sunday school building, which was very rickety and build a new hall, rooms and kitchen. We all helped with fundraising.

In those first years in Knutsford I became interested in the growing Pre-school Playgroup movement and had the idea of starting a playgroup on church premises once the new rooms were built. With this in mind I went with a neighbour on a playgroup leaders course and talked with other young mums and members of the church.

One woman – Barbara – that I talked to was very keen and had been involved in helping in a playgroup in Essex. She had many practical ideas and experience but she didn't want to be Supervisor. Once the building was completed we approached the Church Council and the local Council to get permission to start.

Many people helped us to work towards the start of the playgroup. I was able to involve my father-in-law in making several items of equipment. He was quite handy with woodwork.

Barbara and I started the playgroup together. At first we were allowed up to 14 children. Behind us we had a very capable committee and treasurer. After a very short time we had our fourteen children and a waiting list, so we applied to increase our numbers.

To do this we would need another member of staff. This was one thing, which I made a matter of special prayer, with three people working together – particularly women- you need to really get on. Several people were suggested but none seemed to fit the bill or were unavailable then one Sunday morning I almost literally bumped into Olive. I found myself saying, "Oh Olive, I'm so glad I've seen you we're hoping to increase the number of children in playgroup and we're looking for another helper. Would you be interested?"

I was pleased when she said, "that's something I'd love to do and I'm not working at the moment."

"That's brilliant," I replied, "I'll talk to Barbara and the committee and we'll be in touch."

Olive was a great asset to the playgroup. The Playgroup gained a good reputation in the town and is still running.

CHAPTER THREE

Getting to know the
Person and Power of the Holy Spirit

There must be more to being a Christian than this!

*'John the Baptist said,"I baptize with water but he (Jesus)
will baptize you with the Holy Spirit.'* Mark 1 verse 8

Starting and running the playgroup gave me great satisfaction. That commitment and the family kept me busy but I was still spiritually
discontented and questioning my faith. The things that had first bothered me at Broxbourne continued to perplex me. I knew God was active
in my life and going to church was a lifetime habit. My daily Bible reading and prayer time were still a priority although sometimes the only
peace I got was if I shut myself in the bathroom – we did have two! –
My best friends were in the church too. But still the questions hammered
in my brain, "If the Bible is true and God's promises real why don't I
exhibit the fruit of the Holy Spirit? Why aren't we – the church – healing the sick? Why isn't the church a dynamic growing community like
the early church in Acts?"

The answers to all these questions seemed to be bound up in the power
of the Holy Spirit and I had asked for his power many times. All
Christians had the Holy Spirit anyway didn't they?

It was at this very questioning time in my Christian life, late in 1972
that Bob came to me after morning service. We'd met Bob and his wife
Millicent soon after we arrived in Knutsford at a welcome meeting they
had held in their home for newcomers. We liked them both but didn't
know them very well.

"I wondered if you would like to read this book, I found it very interesting, it's about the Holy Spirit." He said.

With this, he handed me a copy of *Nine O'Clock in the Morning* by Dennis Bennett.

I said, "thanks" took it gladly and then our conversation was interrupted. Why he chose me I don't know; I can only assume that it was God's guidance.

That very afternoon I began devouring the book. Dennis Bennett was an Episcopalian Minister in the USA and he tells of his experience of being 'baptized in the Holy Spirit' It was many years later when I read Dennis Bennett's obituary that I discovered an unexpected link with him. He was English and had come from Ponders End where my father had been born and brought up. This is within about 3 miles, as the crow flies, of where I was born and brought up.

The title of the book comes from the account in Acts 2, of the outpouring of the Holy Spirit at Pentecost. The time it happened was 9 o'clock in the morning. He tells how he met people who had experienced this 'baptism in the Holy Spirit with speaking in tongues' today. Their lives seemed to radiate power and joy. He and his wife wanted and received this baptism in the Holy Spirit with 'speaking in tongues' for themselves.

As I read on, excitement mounted, as the story of their experiences of the supernatural gifts of the Holy Spirit of speaking in tongues and its sister gifts of interpreting tongues, prophecy, discernment, word of knowledge, word of wisdom, faith, healing, power to work miracles, unfolded. He tells the whole story including the problems they encountered because of this experience and it's outworking in his life and ministry.

Despite my busy life I managed to read that book in less than a week and I knew that this was the reality that I had been looking for, I wanted to experience this baptism of the Holy Spirit for myself. That Saturday night I went to my bedroom, David was watching Match of the Day. I sat in bed and just simply asked Jesus to baptize me with the Holy Spirit. I knew he had done it as the words I was praying in changed into a language that I didn't know or understand. I was 'speaking in tongues'. It was a very quiet, simple experience, I was not hysterical or ecstatic just quietly praying in bed, but it changed my life forever!

Life in the Spirit

*'But when the Holy Spirit comes upon you, you will be filled
with power and you will be witnesses for me in Jerusalem, in
all Judaea and Samaria, and to the ends of the earth.'*
Acts 1 verse 8

In the days that followed I knew something special had happened, I knew
Jesus was ALIVE! Prayer. praise, worship and the Bible took on a whole
new reality, a new dimension, a new depth, and yet at the same time simplicity, which has stayed ever since. Ordinary services and sermons in
church seemed charged with meaning and there was hardly ever a boring
sermon. God spoke to me through many parts of the services, hymns,
readings and prayers.

At that time I knew no one else (or so I thought) who had been baptized in the Holy Spirit. I was in for a surprise because when I gave the
book back to Bob he said; "I was baptized in the Holy Spirit earlier this
year"

I looked at him in amazement and said, "I was last night!"

He had told no one else in our church until that moment. Praise God
for Bob's willingness to share with me that day!

So began for me the most exciting time of my Christian life. Trying
so hard to be a Christian changed to trusting – though I am still tempted
to slip back into trying from time to time. I found a new freedom in
praise and worship. Witnessing to my faith became a joy instead of a
chore and opportunities opened without me seeking them. I even dared
to pray with people for healing and some were healed.

One surprising thing that happened to me just after I was filled with
the Holy Spirit was that I could not sleep. Night after night for nearly
two months I slept very fitfully. Until this time if I missed out on sleep,
I would be very bad tempered and find it difficult to cope. This time it
was different; unable to sleep I would lay and pray in 'tongues'. Next day,
although I felt tired, in God's strength I was able to cope.

One day when I was talking to my Christian friend Margaret (she had
been baptized in the Holy Spirit soon after me) I said, "I really don't
know what to do, ever since I've been filled with the Holy Spirit I've
been having trouble sleeping."

"Have you thought of telling the devil to go in Jesus' name?" she asked. "It's him who's trying to keep you awake."

This was something else we found that, as Jesus had become very real to us through receiving the power of the Holy Spirit so, also we were more able to recognize the work of the devil. This is the gift of discernment of spirits, which is one of the gifts mentioned in 1 Corinthians 14. So I thought Margaret's suggestion was worth a try.

That night I did exactly what Margaret had suggested and slept like a baby! As I look back on this experience I see it as a kind of test – a temptation experience – like Jesus had in the wilderness only to a lesser degree.

Before long, there were a few of us in our church who had experienced baptism in the Holy Spirit so we met together to pray and allow God to speak to us through the gifts of the Holy Spirit.

We heard of a charismatic prayer group held regularly at the home of a Methodist minister Rev. Dr Bill Davies, in Padgate near Warrington and we went across as often as we could. A charismatic prayer group is one where the 'charismata' – the gifts of the Holy Spirit are in operation. Most of these gifts are listed in 1 Corinthians 12–14. They are prophecy, speaking in tongues with interpretation, words of knowledge, wisdom, visions, faith, healing, miracles and discernment of spirits.

Sometimes these meetings were joyful with singing, clapping and raising our hands, at other times they were quiet and full of the sense of the presence and holiness of God. The worship would often come to a climax when we sang in tongues. (St Paul calls it singing in or with the Holy Spirit) This is when the Holy Spirit gives you not only the words to speak but also the tune to sing. Each one sings as the spirit leads and the most beautiful harmonies are sung. The singing finishes almost abruptly as though conducted, which in a way it is, by the Holy Spirit.

The first prayer meetings we held in Knutsford itself were at 7 a.m. and I just wouldn't miss them for anything. That was a miracle as I am not a morning person. David is always the one who is up and bouncing around first thing in the morning. He is so cheerful, whistling and singing round the house that I complain and cover my ears. On these prayer meeting mornings though, nothing would keep me in bed.

Later we transferred them to an evening when they would often go on very late, but with Jesus in our midst, who wanted to leave?

Reactions

'For we cannot help speaking about what we have seen and heard.' Acts 4 verse 20

We were so excited by the experience of baptism in the Holy Spirit that we talked to many people in the church and outside about it and lent them books to help them to understand.

A few received this blessing for themselves but others reacted against it. I think some of them thought we had religious mania and avoided us like the plague. Others felt we were saying they were second-class because we had experienced something they hadn't.

I found some of their reactions and attitudes difficult to take. All I wanted to do was to tell people that maybe they had not experienced all that God wanted to give them. Many of them I knew as dedicated Christians but the baptism in the Holy Spirit with the sign of speaking in tongues was not generally preached as being available today, in our church. The baptism in the Holy Spirit came as a totally alien doctrine to them. David at first accepted the idea of Baptism in the Holy Spirit but then viewed it rather suspiciously for a long time.

I'm sure that the 'speaking in tongues' bit put a lot of people off because this has somehow become understood as something weird, ecstatic or hysterical. The New English Bible translation of 'ecstatic utterance' doesn't do much for the image!

Some people argued theologically that it just couldn't happen the way we had experienced it, or said that it wasn't for today. My theology follows from my experience not the other way round! Theology is, after all, people's understanding of God. I had experienced something new of God. Nobody could say it hadn't happened because it didn't fit in with his or her pet theory.

I was driven back to the Bible and there I found our experience to be completely biblical. Jesus himself had been born of the Holy Spirit at his birth and then empowered by the Holy Spirit for his ministry at his water baptism. There are several examples in the Acts of the Apostles of this second experience of empowering with the Holy Spirit from Pentecost in Acts chapter 2 onwards. On most occasions the experience is accompanied by speaking in tongues as well.

In Acts chapter 9 we find Ananias going to Saul three days after his conversion on the Damascus road. He is sent to lay hands on Saul for healing of the blindness that had afflicted him at his conversion and also for him to receive the Holy Spirit. There is no mention that Saul spoke in tongues at that point but we do know that he did speak in tongues because he says so in 1 Corinthians chapter 14 v 18.

The story of some Samaritans receiving the Holy Spirit is recorded in Acts chapter 8 v 14. Again there is no mention of speaking in tongues but something unusual happened.

The Gentile believers in Cornelius' household received the Holy Spirit and spoke in tongues. The whole story of Gods planning in Acts chapter 10 is worth reading.

A further example is found in Acts chapter 19 verses 1–7 where some Ephesians receive the Holy Spirit together with speaking in tongues and prophecy.

There is also fully documented evidence of this happening throughout the history of the Christian Church.

I did feel, with some people, that they argued theologically to avoid being faced with the challenge of experiencing it. I can understand that such a very real experience of God can seem threatening. But a God whose very name is love will never do anything to harm us.

We issued invitations for people to join us at our prayer meetings. They were never 'hole in the corner'. Few took us up on it. Rumours and stories about what went on there were many and varied. People were even warned to keep away from us by a local vicar!

What we didn't realize at first was that people in many of the more traditional churches, not just the Pentecostal ones, around the country and also in many parts of the world, were experiencing the baptism in the Holy Spirit too.

We certainly made mistakes in our enthusiasm. However, the devil used every opportunity to lie and deceive people and pervert the truth. He did not want people to accept the Holy Spirit. We are too powerful and much more of a threat to him when we are filled with the Holy Spirit.

Going on in the Spirit

*'And these signs will accompany those who believe; In my
name they will drive out demons; they will speak in new
tongues; they will pick up snakes with their hands; and when
they drink deadly poison, it will not hurt them at all; they
will place their hands on sick people and they will get well.'*
Mark 16 verses 17–18

The group of people who had been filled with the Holy Spirit and now
met together were like the disciples, very diverse and there were differences of opinion, temperament and outlook between us. It seemed at
times, that God was grinding us against each other to make us into living
stones built together. (1 Peter 2 v 5)

Whatever the differences between us and others' reactions to us, God
continued to bless us with his presence. He answered prayers for individuals and the group. He spoke to us in many ways. Prayers for healing
were offered and we saw miracles before our eyes.

One evening we had a visitor who had a healing ministry for lengthening legs. Many people have one leg longer than the other, which can
cause back pain and other problems. It is impossible to see a miracle of
say, healing a stomach ulcer, but lengthening a leg we should be able to
see. As he prayed with two different people I watched and saw the leg
'grow' resulting in the relief of long term back pain.

It was from this group that we watched the first chapters of the
F.G.B.M.F.I. (Full Gospel Business Mens Fellowship International) in
this country inaugurated. This is an American organization founded for
the evangelisation of men. They hold breakfast and dinner meetings
where a meal and testimony is shared. They also have a magazine called
'Voice' which is full of individual testimonies that are very encouraging.

Travelling one day to pray with someone for healing Margaret and I
had a wonderful experience of God's provision. As we set off from
Knutsford Margaret said "I really must get some petrol in Macclesfield,
the gauge is hovering around empty and there aren't any petrol stations
till we get to Whaley Bridge."

We travelled on chattering away (as women do!) and completely forgot about the petrol until we were right out into the hills. What could

we do? Margaret had a gift of faith and believed that God would supply the petrol to get us to the next town. We spent the next few miles, up hill and down dale, praying and praising until we arrived in Whaley Bridge on an empty tank. (For the sceptics amongst us there was no reserve tank in that car.)

We were blessed in one of our Tuesday evening meetings when one member had a vision of Jesus going round the circle of praying people laying his hand on each head in blessing.

Another vision (though I prefer to call it a picture), which blessed us, was given to Margaret and I when we were praying for her eldest son Stephen. He was at University then and wanted a job for part of the vacation. As we prayed I got a picture of a mushroom in my mind that wouldn't go away. I was hungry and it was nearly lunchtime but why a mushroom? Eventually, I said to Margaret "I have this picture in my mind of a mushroom". Even as I shared this I remembered that there is a mushroom farm about 3 miles from where we live.

Stephen telephoned them straight away to ask if they had any holiday jobs this conversation followed:

Stephen, "Have you any holiday jobs for students?"

Voice on the other end of the 'phone, "How did you know we had a job we haven't advertised it yet!"

Stephen, a Christian himself, told the story. I don't know whether they believed him or not when he explained. The timing was perfect. The job lasted for just over three weeks, which was the only time Stephen had free for work that summer.

On another occasion Margaret's husband Bob was due to go to Japan on business. Every time it was mentioned I got the word 'earthquake' in my mind. Supposing it was a prophetic word or a word of knowledge? It frightened me. I tried to dismiss it from my mind but one Tuesday evening it was there again. I shared my word with the group and we were able to pray for protection on Bob whilst he was in Japan. There was an earthquake while he was there. The trains and other travel were disrupted but Bob was kept safe. Praise the Lord!

I was still working at the playgroup and there was one particular boy I found difficult to handle. There seemed to be a clash of personalities. I was so frustrated one day that I went home and really prayed about it.

(Why do we make prayer a last resort?) Once I prayed I forgot about it till next morning. The lad in question was the first to arrive and he came bounding into the room and threw himself into my arms and hugged me. In that instant my attitude changed – God had given me a deep love for that child.

One woman, Dorothy, came along to the fellowship with her son who had pains in his chest. Doctors had been unable to find a cause for these pains. He was healed through prayer over a long period of time and became a Christian too.

His mother was to teach us many lessons. She became ill with depression, which was so bad that her husband would leave her sitting in a chair when he went to work in the morning and find her still there when he returned in the evening. We prayed with her in the group and in her home. We prayed when she went into hospital or saw a doctor that she would have the right treatment. She did get a lot better but has had relapses since, but her faith remains strong.

What is Speaking in Tongues?

'All of them were filled with the Holy Spirit and began to
speak in other tongues as the spirit enabled them.'
Acts 2 verse 4

After I was baptized in the Holy Spirit I had many conversations with folk about my experience but the gift of speaking in tongues was a sticking point with some of them. They thought it was peculiar and yet, as this is often the first gift to be given, it needs to be understood. A typical conversation with a friend (I'll call her Jane) would go like this:

Jane: I'd love to be baptized with the Holy Spirit but I don't want to speak in tongues.

Me: Why not?

Jane: It's rather weird, you're in a trance when you speak in tongues. You're out of control, I don't like being out of control.

Me: You're not in a trance at all. It's true you don't actually know what you're saying unless God gives you the interpretation as well, but you can decide whether to speak or not.

Jane: So what's the point of it? It doesn't make sense if you don't know what you're saying. At least at Pentecost people around understood what the disciples were saying, but that doesn't happen today.

Me: It does still happen today just last week my daughter told me of how two of her friends were praying together and one spoke in tongues and the other understood it. It was Portuguese, which the one praying had never learned but the other had!

Jane: Wow, that's amazing! But what's the point of it if other people can't understand it?

Me: Well it's often a confirmation sign that you've been baptized in the Holy Spirit – it was for me.

Jane: I'd much rather have one of the other gifts – healing would be lovely.

Me; It's not a case of either or, I believe that if we need any of the gifts as we work for God then it will be there for us to use – they're tools. Anyway, tongues often comes as part of the package, it did at Pentecost – the disciples didn't ask for it, it just happened and it was just like that for me? Do you think God's going to give you something to harm you or that isn't any use?

Jane: Put like that, I suppose not. It does say in Luke that he won't give us a snake if we ask for a fish, or a scorpion if we ask for an egg, so I suppose not. But I still don't know what it's for.

Me: Well, sometimes people speak out in a meeting and then there's an interpretation it's a bit like prophecy.

Jane: Why doesn't God just give someone a prophecy?

Me: I don't know, perhaps he wants two people to exercise their faith – God is God!

Jane: Can you use it in any other way?

Me: St Paul says it's for edification – it builds up the person praying. I find it useful when I'm praying for other people too. It's difficult to know how to pray sometimes, isn't it?

Jane; All the time! So you can use speaking in tongues in intercession?

Me: Yes, it's brilliant – and in praise and worship too, – have you ever heard singing in tongues?

Jane: I'm not sure, I did once hear what sounded like a wonderful choir in a prayer and praise meeting, but I couldn't understand what they were singing – then it finished quite suddenly.

Me: Sounds like that's what you heard – the Holy Spirit was the conductor, that's why it stopped so suddenly. God gives the words and the tune. Isn't it St Paul who says we should pray without ceasing? The only way I could do that is if I prayed in tongues – because you don't have to think about it. It's brilliant for praying while you're driving.

Jane: There's a lot more to this speaking in tongues than I thought.

Me: One thing I hope is that God uses this gift to control what I use my tongue for <u>all</u> the time not just when I speak in tongues – it's so easy to hurt people with what you say and you can't take words back.

Jane: Words can be very hurtful.

Me: Some words – good and bad – stay with us forever. Have you ever thought how your voice is one thing that no one else can use?

Jane: That would be real commitment if I allowed God to use my voice. - Suppose I ask you to pray with me now to be baptized with the Holy Spirit and I start speaking in tongues, how will I know I'm not making it up?

Me: Well it's a step of faith. Experiments have been done, though – they reckon that no one can make up more than a few words – unless, of course, they've been filled with the Holy Spirit – then the words will be what God has given them! Have you ever heard of Jackie Pullinger and David Wilkerson?

Jane: Wasn't Jackie the woman who went to Hong Kong and ministered to the drug addicts?

Me: Yes, that's right and David Wilkerson had a ministry to the gangs in New York both tell of how they prayed in tongues as they walked around and how it seemed to lead them to people who wanted to know about Jesus – so it must be pretty powerful.

Sometimes these conversations led on to receiving the Holy Spirit and speaking in tongues but sometimes sadly, people turned away.

CHAPTER FOUR

Learning Obedience

Called to Preach

'He took me from caring for my flock and told me to go and prophesy.' Amos 7 verse 15

In one Sunday morning service our minister took the lesson in the Old Testament from Amos chapter 7. The verse that became important for me was verse 15, which in the Good News Bible says *'He took me from caring for my flock and told me to go and prophesy'*. It impressed itself on me and stayed with me. A week or two later the verse came in our family prayer schedule, then it came again in my own daily reading. It cropped up several times over the course of some months. I was sure that God was trying to speak to me, but what was he saying.

I was feeling unsettled in my playgroup work and wondering if I should give it up. Could it be that the 'flock' mentioned in the text were the playgroup children? After more prayer and consideration I decided that God was saying that, so I gave in my notice at playgroup.

But what did the second half of the text mean? What did *'go and prophesy'* mean for me? Occasionally I have been used to give a prophecy or 'word from the Lord' in a meeting, but this did not seem to be enough to fulfil this instruction. Then, within the space of a few weeks, three ministers outside our own circuit suggested independently "Shouldn't you be preaching?"

In the Methodist church we have what are called 'Local Preachers' – David has been one since soon after we married.

Now I found myself in a dilemma. I had a growing conviction that I should become a preacher but I had bad reactions from people I respected. They quoted St Paul's teaching *'Women should not teach men'* and *'women should keep silence in Church'* (1 Timothy 2 v 12) at me. The

Methodist Church accepts women as Local Preachers and ordained ministers too. My husband had no problem with it – he was full of encouragement.

Despite the external pressures the inner conviction grew. I knew I had to be obedient. I tested the call by offering to the Church as a Local Preacher and was taken 'on note', the first stage in the training process.

I went forward in obedience to God but I still needed to settle once and for all how I understood Scripture and how I could reconcile St Paul's apparent contradiction about women's place. Wherever the Bible is taken literally this subject comes up. What does God allow women to do in the Church?

The teaching about how men and women should behave in church is mainly found in 1 Timothy 2 v 8–14. If we are to take note of women keeping silence in church and not teaching men then perhaps men should take note of St Paul's injunction to '*lift up holy hands when praying*'. We need to balance one set of teaching against another because in Galatians 3 v 28 St Paul also says '*There is neither Jew nor Greek, slave nor free, male or female, for you are all one in Christ Jesus.*'

St Paul teaches about many things, one of which is the behaviour of slaves, in fact there is more teaching about slaves than about women. (see Ephesians 6 v 5–9 and the book of Philemon). If we are going to enforce the teaching of Paul on how women should behave, then should we not also accept the teaching about how slaves should behave? When the abolition of slavery was mooted some people did oppose it because of Scripture, but who now would try to enforce St Paul's teaching on slavery? Do you consider slavery to be right? Should we then continue with the bondage of women?

In our churches most congregations are made up of two thirds women and one third men. This being the case, how can we hope to get all our leaders and teachers from amongst the third that happen to be men? Especially as most of the men, are involved in full time work and a career.

Yonggi Cho in Seoul, Korea, the pastor of the largest and fastest growing church in the world, has women as 60% of his leaders. He used the people who were available and willing. His church is still growing.

I wonder how many women there are throughout the world who are frustrated and also in a state of disobedience to God because of the enforcement of this rigid doctrine of women not taking any sort of lead in the Church? The devil must be clapping his hands because of the large mainly untapped spiritual resources there are within the women in these fellowships and churches.

At times people are still antagonistic towards me as a woman preacher, but knowing it is God's will for me, I am content. When he calls us he expects us to obey him and then he will equip us to do the work.

I now knew why God had called me out of playgroup I needed the time to study for the Local Preachers exams. I had done very little study since leaving school so I didn't find the exams and practical work easy. Once I got into it I enjoyed it and found the practical preaching rewarding.

At the end of my studies I had to conduct a trial service and also take an oral examination. The oral examination was taken at the Local Preachers meeting and I knew I would have to give testimony particularly about my call to preach. I was very apprehensive about this because my call to preach was very much tied up with the baptism in the Holy Spirit I had experienced. I knew through previous conversations that some of the preachers did not approve of my kind of experience. However, God encouraged me by reminding me of Mark 13 v 11 *'Don't worry beforehand about what to say. Just say whatever is given you at the time, for it is not you speaking, but the Holy Spirit.'* I don't remember much about what I said at that oral exam but He got me through.

It took me three years to complete my studies to become a fully accredited Local Preacher and the final hurdle was the service of recognition. In this service the preacher has to make promises to God and the church. Since I have been filled with the Holy Spirit I have had a much wider view of the church than one denomination. I see the church, the body of Christ, as all 'born again' believers. As I read the promises the week before the service I felt they were much too narrow, promising allegiance to 'the Methodist Church'.

I prayed and pondered the matter with a growing uneasiness until I decided to ring our Superintendent Minister.

"I'm having difficulty with one of the promises I have to make in the recognition service." I said. "It's the one where I promise to serve God in the Methodist Church. I feel it's far too narrow and confining and I can't in all honesty promise that to God. I see the church as much wider than the Methodist Church. Please could you alter it slightly to widen it?"

The reply was and uncompromising "No, it's the standard service. If you can't make that promise you can't become a local preacher."

My heart sank, was all that work to be for nothing? What about my call from God? Had I been mistaken? Strangely I had peace, I knew I couldn't make that promise as it stood. It was God's problem not mine. If my way to Methodist preaching were blocked, then God would have to open another way.

I rang another Minister I knew outside our Circuit and told him my dilemma and asked "What can I do?"

His response was encouraging as he said, "There's a new order for the recognition service out now and that promise is phrased differently. Why don't you ask if you can use the new format?"

I rang off and rang our Superintendent. Again the way was blocked, the order of worship had been printed and he would not change it.

It was later on the Saturday when I heard from our minister again saying, "I'm not prepared to take anything away from the promise but I will add just a few words."

I don't remember exactly what they were, but these words widened the promise and made it possible for me to make that promise to the church and to God. The service went forward without any further hitch and the Church confirmed the call I had received from God.

Some Perils of Preaching – Early Experiences

'Preach the Word; be prepared in season and out of season;
correct, rebuke and encourage – with great patience and
careful instruction.' 2 Timothy 4 verse 2

Once out on the Circuit I soon discovered that preaching could have it's lighter side. It can sometimes be quite embarrassing too, for instance, one Mothering Sunday morning I had chosen as my topic Mary the mother of Jesus and as I sang the second hymn I found myself singing lustily, instead of 'most highly favoured lady' most highly <u>flavoured</u> lady! I had the hardest job to restrain my laughter. To make matters worse, immediately after the hymn we took the offering and as I stood holding the plate to bless it I looked down to see nestling among the notes and coins one trouser button. We were at that time in the middle of a recession – but a trouser button?

Telling my husband afterwards he said, "You'd do anything to spice up your services!"

Nowadays when you preach you don't usually suffer the problems of early preachers, heckling, pelting with fruit, vegetables or stones – even imprisonment and death. In this country you can usually preach in safety and peace. Sometimes, let's face it, it's all too peaceful, like when I preach on Sunday afternoons and at least one of the well fed congregation falls asleep or they even take it in turns. One day I shall overcome my inhibitions and shout, "the children of Israel are asleep!"

My husband (as you know also a preacher) once had to suffer a rather eccentric man sitting right at the front of the church not only sleeping but also snoring loudly with his false teeth grinning up at him from the hymnbook shelf! Perhaps it says more about the preachers than the congregations.

One effect nerves has on me is not cold feet but cold hands that is fine until I shake hands at the door after the service.

I like to arrive at a church at least fifteen minutes before the service is due to start, arriving at one town church we were all locked out until a resourceful steward tracked down a key at the last moment.

At a country chapel again arriving in good time I found the chapel open but not a soul in sight. Everyone, including the organist appeared, as if out of the woodwork, just one minute before the service was due to start.

While I was still 'on trial' as a preacher my husband came with me and sat towards the back of the chapel. He was incensed to hear a stage whisper from the back row "I'm deaf, very poor, can't hear a word!"

On tackling the woman afterwards and suggesting that perhaps she should sit nearer the front, she replied, "But I always sit here!" Who can argue with that kind of logic?

One health hazard you face is that of the carafe or glass of water in the pulpit. My husband has it down to a fine art and asks if there is any fresh water in the pulpit. I always mean to ask but usually forget. Once in the pulpit there is the carafe of water looking distinctly green, or a half empty not too clean glass. How long has it been there? How many unsuspecting preachers have already drunk from it? Dare I risk drinking from it? If in doubt I pray that my voice lasts out without needing lubrication.

One chapel I regularly visit has a schoolroom attached with a flimsy partition between. As the service progresses you can hear Junior Church singing their hymns. On one memorable occasion I found myself competing with a full-scale practice of 'Joseph and his Amazing Technicolor Dreamcoat'.

We used to preach at a centre where many of the people are mentally retarded. This could be a joy, as they are mostly like children, but one Sunday I used a bee as an illustration (I can't now remember exactly what it illustrated!) One lady got this bee in her bonnet and kept interrupting me to talk about it for the rest of the service. Even the prayers were not spared her interruption.

It is an encouragement at the end of a service when someone says that God has spoken to him or her through the service, but something that happened several years ago still makes my hair stand on end.

I decided to preach about forgiveness, taking the two aspects, God's forgiveness of us and our forgiveness of other people. As I shook hands at the door one person and then another asked me "How did you know?" Eventually, when someone I knew quite well in the congregation came out and asked me the same question, I asked, "How did I know what?" It was then that I was told that there had been a schism in the church that week and the greatest need was for forgiveness on both sides.

I didn't know what had been going on but God did and I was touched and amazed by His wonderful guidance.

One thing is certain it is a joy, a privilege and a responsibility to preach, but essential tools as you travel around are adaptability and a sense of humour.

Baptism of another kind – this time water

'Peter said, repent and be baptized, every one of you, in the
name of Jesus Christ for the forgiveness of your sins.'
Acts 2 verse 38.

As my faith continued to deepen and grow, over a period of several months, the subject of baptism in water for repentance kept cropping up. I had been baptized as an infant, which is the Methodist way, but now it seemed that God wanted more from me. Slowly the conviction grew that I should be baptized by total immersion. Scripturally baptism was carried out as a sign of repentance and I could hardly say I had repented as a baby. The tradition for infant baptism grew up from the early church because when someone was baptized it would be 'so and so and his entire household', which included babies, children and probably slaves as well.

I kept getting a 'nudge' until one day, I realized afresh, that Jesus himself had been baptized by John the Baptist. Jesus had no need of repentance, he was sinless but he was baptized nevertheless. If Jesus thought it right then it was good enough for me.

One Tuesday evening at the prayer meeting the subject of baptism came up and several people there said they were feeling like me, that they needed 'believers baptism'. We began to think how we could arrange it. Most of us belonged to the Methodist Church, so it could cause problems for our minister. We had to do it God's way.

Later that summer, while some of the fellowship went off to a Christian camp, we went as a family to Haldon Court at Exmouth. Haldon Court is a Christian holiday centre. We had a good time of fellowship. The children loved it, as there were lots of other children to play with together with sports facilities and a swimming pool.

On Thursday evening an announcement was made, "A lady has asked if we would be prepared to baptize her in the swimming pool. We have agreed to do this tomorrow afternoon and if anyone else would like to be baptized please let us know."

From that moment I had a tussle within myself. We had been trying to plan something together from the fellowship – that way, we reasoned, we would be a witness to other people, however, God seemed to be speaking very clearly and quietly within me, telling me that it was a matter between Him and me. It came down to obedience, whatever the others were going to do didn't matter; God wanted me to be baptized.

I spoke to David, "Do you mind if I'm baptized tomorrow?"

"Why do you need to be baptized? he asked, "You've already been baptized as a baby."

This was the kind of comment I had had from within the Methodist

Church and I understood why they said it but still felt that God was saying something different to me personally.

"I know," I said, "but I feel that this is what God wants me to do and if that's what He wants then I want to be obedient. It's such a good opportunity and won't cause a problem to anyone in the church."

David didn't question any more just accepted my decision.

There were seven of us in all who were baptized that afternoon. We each gave a short testimony first. I can swim, but I'm not too happy about getting my face underwater, so I was apprehensive about going right under. It was a quick dunk then it was all over, I did not have time to be afraid and remember my baptism with joy. Water baptism symbolizes death to the old life and the beginning of a new life in Christ. God had provided another new beginning.

When I came home from holiday and shared my experience with the fellowship, they too had something to share – some of them had been baptized at the Christian camp. Their baptism had taken place in a chilly river, I was glad mine had been in a warm swimming pool! God's planning and timing are amazing. This incident showed me just how much God is interested in each individual and how important it is to be obedient.

On the move again

'The Glory of the latter house shall be greater than the former and my peace shall be upon it.' Haggai 2 verse 9
(Authorised Version.)

We had been living in Knutsford for about 4 years and, although we liked Knutsford, and our house, it had one major drawback; it backed on to a noisy main road. We had talked about moving but never very seriously. Then some neighbours who lived on the other side of the cul-de-sac put their house up for sale. It was exactly the same design as ours but much better situated with a south-facing garden and away from the main road.

As soon as it came on the market David wanted to buy it. I argued with him. It seemed to me that, if we were to move at all, it would make more sense to move nearer to the centre of the town and the children's school so that we would be able to walk everywhere rather than using the car all the time. David was adamant. He made an offer for the house and it was accepted, now all we had to do was to sell our own. This was to prove difficult and we had a bridging loan for 15 months.

I continued to pray about the situation, finally accepting what I could not change. I do believe that in a family the man has the final say on any contentious issue, although I thought in this case he was wrong. I relinquished the matter to the Lord and only then got peace of mind and began to plan for the move.

We were due to move on Monday and as usual went to Church on Sunday morning. The preacher that morning was an elderly visiting preacher from a neighbouring circuit. When he announced his text I nearly fell off the pew! It was from Haggai chapter 2 and verse 9 in the authorized version of the Bible: *'The glory of the latter house shall be greater than the former and my peace shall be upon it.'* Until that morning I had no idea that there was such a text in the Bible – the fact that the preacher decided to preach on it that particular day was truly amazing. Once more God's timing was perfect. I couldn't tell you what the sermon was about; I just sat there praising the Lord!

I was unable to thank the preacher for his words that day but did later manage to tell him just how much he had blessed us with that text.

David had been right about the move and God fulfilled His promise for us in that house, not that we were always happy there, but that His peace never left it. Our next-door neighbours became almost like a second set of parents

Early Experiences of Healing

'Preach the message that the kingdom of heaven is near, heal the sick, raise the dead, cleanse those who have leprosy, drive out demons. Freely you have received freely give'.
Matthew 10 verses 17–18.

The lack of the healing ministry within the church was one of the things I had questioned before I was baptized with the Holy Spirit. Every one of us needs healing from time to time and many people suffer. When you suffer or feel compassion for those who suffer you want to do something. Jesus spent a lot of his ministry '*healing all who came to him*'

I soon discovered that now I was filled with the Holy Spirit I had faith to pray with people for healing and saw some wonderful answers to those prayers. I just obeyed the commission of Jesus to '*lay your hands on the sick and they will recover*', and left the results to God. There has always been some blessing if not always physical healing.

On one occasion I had a friend's children staying. She and her husband had gone south to a funeral. It was near to Christmas and I was still working in playgroup when Sally became ill. She had a sore throat, swollen glands and a high temperature. The doctor came to see her but he said, "I can't treat her at the moment, I'm not sure whether she has tonsillitis or glandular fever. Antibiotics would cure the tonsillitis but they would do nothing for the glandular fever. We'll have to see how it develops."

That night the visiting boys were sleeping in her room so Sally was in with us. From time to time I woke to hear her moaning in her delirium. In the early hours of the morning I became conscious once more, of her moans. As I lay there, into my mind dropped the Bible reference Matthew chapter 8 v 9. At the time I used the Living Bible and I quietly got out of bed and took my Bible to the light to read what it said. The end of the verse says '*you have the authority to tell the sickness to go and it will go*'. I knelt by Sally's bed and said "I tell this sickness to go from Sally now in the name of Jesus!" and it went. The following day she bounced out of bed and went happily (or at least as happily as she ever did!) to school.

Sometimes when we prayed it seemed that the Lord said 'no' or we blocked his healing in some way. My youngest uncle became ill with cancer and Margaret Boler and I went across to Newark to pray with him on two occasions, but sadly he died.

An area of my own body, which needed healing, were my kidneys, during pregnancy and after Sally was born I had a lot of infections. After the diagnosis of a congenital deformity discovered through X-ray I was put on a course of pills, one each day which the doctor inferred I would have to take for the rest of my life. I took them without question and went back for regular check ups. I was still doing this when I moved to Knutsford.

Some time after I'd been baptized in the Holy Spirit I felt convinced that I should stop taking the tablets. (I don't recommend that to anyone else. You have to be really sure of God's guidance about it first.) I knew that the worst that could happen in my case would be a urine infection and I would have my usual check up in 3 months anyway.

I went back for my check up and had the usual test. It was perfectly all right, no infection. Then I confessed to the doctor what I had done (or rather had not done!) His comment made me think. "Well," he said, "it hasn't done you any harm has it? Anyway they've changed the treatment for your kind of condition and only give medication if there is a urinary infection."

Would I have found that out if I hadn't stopped taking the tablets? Or would I still be taking them I wonder? I don't take the tablets now and seldom have infections.

I had a recurring problem with sinusitis; it had been with me since I was in my teens. Prayer would relieve the symptoms but it recurred and I would need another batch of anti-biotics. I saw a consultant and was scheduled for an operation to remove some polyps and wash out my sinuses. I asked for prayer from our prayer chain and they prayed that I would receive the best treatment. I went in dread to the hospital (I'm scared of operations), only to be sent home and told to await recall. The porters and ancillary workers strike was on and they couldn't cope with all the admissions and operations.

Within a week or two we had news that David's firm had enrolled us as a family in a private health care scheme. They accepted me into the scheme, sinusitis and all. Under this scheme I saw a different specialist and he recommended a similar operation, which was carried out at a hospital nearer my home. I hate the evening before an operation; there is a feeling of fear knowing that you will be completely out of control of what happens to you. I've had several operations and I always feel the same. I can say (and <u>know</u>) that God is in charge but I still <u>feel</u> afraid.) This operation proved to be a great success although it was very painful at first.

One thing I have prayed about often is that I have no sense of smell. Though my husband assures me that this can be a positive advantage at times, I would love to smell the flowers and food cooking etc. Perhaps God will heal me one day.

Because I know what it is like to be ill I am sensitive to how some people live daily with pain. I noticed in our local press that there was to be a series of spiritualist healing meetings in Knutsford. When you are ill you will do anything to get relief and healing so I became concerned. The trouble with going to a spiritualist healer is that you may end up physically healed but with moral, psychological or spiritual problems. When Jesus heals there are no side effects only good ones.

I went to see our minister about my concerns and suggested that we might have healing services at our church. He said "no" As my concerns were still there I asked further afield if I might run a service in one of our small chapels but the way was blocked there too. By one of those wonderful God coincidences – and a friend of a friend, I found people in a country chapel outside our circuit that were happy for me to run a healing meeting there once a week. Margaret and I did this for about a year and saw some wonderful healings, even though we had very small congregations.

One young Mum who came was healed of gynaecological problems and a bad back. More wonderful than that was that she and her mother and eventually the whole family became Christians because of the healing.

We saw another wonderful healing take place through those meetings. A lady came one evening and we prayed for her. It was only later that she told us that she was suffering with a brain tumour and had been given just 3 months to live.

She was still living 6 years later, though we have lost touch with her now.

I called on a neighbour one day "How are you Una?" I asked.

"I've got laryngitis," she whispered, "I don't know what I'm going to do I should be singing in the operatic society's production this evening."

"Oh dear, would you like me to pray for you," I asked.

"Yes please."

I prayed and laid my hands on her and then left. It was about a fortnight later when I saw her again.

"Hallo Una. Are you better?"

"Yes thank you, Your prayer worked I sang that evening and people at the end of the performance even commented on the clarity and power of my voice!"

– Praise the Lord!

My next-door neighbour Verlie had a problem with a knee, which slipped rather easily out of joint causing pain and swelling. Because it happened so readily she was very careful to walk on even ground. I called on the day of her daughter's wedding.

"I'm really worried about my knee," she said, "the church path is rather uneven and I'm afraid it will let me down."

"Would you like me to pray with you?" I asked.

She agreed.

A few days later I saw her and asked, "How did the wedding go?"

"Lovely," she said, "and my knee was fine, in fact I didn't give it a thought all day!"

When Christians pray for healing there can be recriminations. If the person is not healed he may feel that he didn't have enough faith and then feel condemnation as well as still suffering the illness. Then again, the faith or lack of it, of the person ministering healing is important too. Or if it is in a church situation, there can be a faithless attitude in the congregation, which militates against healing. It was even said of Jesus '*he could not perform many miracles in his own home town because of their lack of faith*'. Faith is obviously a key to healing as Jesus said many times '*your faith has healed you or made you whole*' but there should be no one feeling guilt or condemnation after the ministry of healing. There will always be some blessing and God's timing comes into it too.

I believe that we should be faithful in our commission '*to lay our hands on the sick and they will be healed*' and leave the results to God. After all <u>we</u> can't heal anyone it is only Jesus who can do it. If a doctor's patient doesn't get well you don't blame him as long as he did his best. Is it any different for Christian healing?

Bookshops and Prisons

'I was in prison and you came to visit me.'
Matthew 25 verse 36B.

After completing my Local Preaching studies I found myself with time on my hands. The children were older and less demanding but more expensive, so I started looking for a part-time job.

One weekend Jo, a friend from schooldays, and her husband were staying so we went out looking around Knutsford. Jo noticed an advert in the bookshop for part time staff, I applied, had an interview and was soon working 4 mornings a week there.

A few months later a job with some typing became available in their other branch, the Bargain Bookshop, I transferred there. Apart from selling books we serviced the adult fiction for Manchester libraries. I enjoyed that time, the work could be repetitive but we all worked well together and had a lot of laughs.

This was my second experience of the retail trade as when I was 15 and 16 I had a Saturday job in a sweet shop (teenager's heaven?) I worked from 9 a.m. to 5.30 p.m. for nine shillings – my wage after National Insurance had been deducted (but I digress!)

My weekends were busy with preaching and I sang as an alto in a choir. Margaret Boler had formed the choir to perform Jimmy and Carol Owens musical 'Come Together'. Later we re-formed to perform 'The Witness', again by Carol and Jimmy Owens. 'The Witness' is a musical based around Peter's experience of Jesus. It covers the story of Jesus from when he called the disciples and continues through to the Resurrection and the coming of the Holy Spirit. It is a powerful evangelistic tool.

We went to churches and towns but the occasions I remember most were when we went into remand centres and prisons. One evening Kay and I were late arriving at Risley remand centre. The rest of the choir and audience were already in place. We had to walk the length of the hall to the sound of wolf whistles and catcalls …

The effect of 'The Witness' on that audience was powerful there was silence when appropriate and cheers or jeers when appropriate. It ended with tumultuous applause and some men became Christians through it.

We went to sing at Strangeways prison. Approaching the forbidding gates on that freezing February Sunday morning it was not just the cold that made me shiver. It was the first time I'd been inside a prison and we were let in one by one through the main gates, then they clanged shut. Each door we went through was carefully unlocked then securely locked after us once we had all been counted through.

After setting up in the chapel and starting to sing, we were disappointed to see just two rows of prisoners and they soon left. The chaplain

Rev. Noel Proctor encouraged us to carry on singing as he hoped they would come back. The Prison Officers work to rule was on so they never did. We finished 'The Witness' to an empty chapel and the Glory of God. When we finished the chaplain was very apologetic and invited us back once the dispute was over.

We did go back and sang this time to a crowded chapel. The response was very vocal and several of the men became Christians in response to it. Looking at the faces of the men in that prison I thought how young and ordinary they looked.

At the end of each performance Margaret asked a person from the choir to give a word of testimony to what God had done in their life. There can be response to this testimony as well as the musical.

A vicar invited us to Barrow-in-Furness to perform 'The Witness'. The church offered to provide overnight hospitality for us so that we could sing at the church on Sunday as well.

As we gathered after the performance on Saturday evening we were counted and there were two more of us than anticipated and one couple kindly offered two of us hospitality at the last minute. Gloria and I went with this couple. When we went into the bedroom we discovered we were to sleep on bunk beds – they were not very strong and looked as though they were really meant for children. Gloria, although older than me was smaller and slimmer and volunteered to take the top bunk. I don't think either of us slept a wink that night. We both thought we'd end up squashed in a heap!

The choir, 'The Hosanna Singers' continued for a long time after I left, seeing their ministry mostly in prisons.

CHAPTER FIVE

Some Hard Lessons

Five Days of Heaven

'And we know that in all things God works for the good of those who loves Him who have been called according to his purpose.' Romans 8 verse 28. And *'Give thanks in all circumstances.'* 1 Thessalonians 5 verse 18

As we learn more about God and his purposes he teaches us lessons and in 1979 he began teaching me the connection between these two verses. The only way that it is possible to fulfil the second injunction is if you believe in the first. The whole idea seemed like an impossible ideal to me!

It was another of those occasions when it seemed as if I came across these texts everywhere. Then I was lent the book by Merlin Carothers called 'Prison to Praise', which tells of how he learned to praise God <u>in all circumstances</u>. What I saw was that you couldn't give thanks for all circumstances, because not everything that happens to you is good, but you could give thanks **in** all circumstances. There is always something to thank God for, he shows his love to us in so many ways and we can always thank him for His son Jesus dying on the cross for us.

Two incidents that helped me to begin to understand, were, firstly when I was driving on narrow winding roads in Derbyshire and found myself stuck behind a lorry, instead of moaning I thought I would give praising a try. As I was praising God, He told me to pray for the driver. How could I do that, I didn't know his needs? I prayed in 'tongues,' God knew what the driver needed so He could intercede for him. My normal frustration was replaced with a practical concern for the driver. I still do this and sometimes the lorries turn off quickly, at others, they stay in front longer. God knows how much prayer they need.

The second incident happened in my kitchen when I was clearing up after a meal and dropped a large bottle of ketchup on the floor, the bottle broke and glass and ketchup splattered everywhere! Instead of my usual angry outburst I said "Praise the Lord!" As I heard these words come from my lips I roared with laughter. The situation had not changed. I still had to clear up a sticky dangerous mess, but my attitude had been transformed.

Another lesson I was relearning was of generous giving (Mum had been my first teacher) *'The Lord loves a generous giver'.* We had a garden large enough to grow some vegetables and soon after we'd moved in Pop planted 3 rhubarb crowns and they flourished. It was the beginning of the rhubarb season so I went to pull some. I took it inside and there was 7lbs. I prepared some for our pudding and was going to continue and put the rest in the freezer. I felt a 'nudge' to give it away, so I did.

Less than a week later Pop asked "Do you want me to pull some rhubarb?"

Expecting a few mean stalks I said, "Yes, please."

Imagine my surprise when a few minutes later in came another 7lbs. I know rhubarb can grow quickly but I knew how little had been left after the first picking! Since then we have given away pounds of rhubarb and at least 15 crowns and we still have plenty.

Many times meals have stretched to feed unexpected visitors or I've found myself buying extra things at the supermarket and then someone has turned up to eat them.

It was in February 1979 that, Martin, then 15 went to hear the Christian music group 'Living Sound' at Macclesfield. He went with the Youth Group from our church. We waited up for him and I asked, "was it good?"

"It was excellent. They made an appeal at the end and I nearly went forward."

The following day was half-term and after breakfast Martin said, "I'm going out for a walk. I have some thinking to do. I could be out for a long time but don't worry."

He was out from just after 9 till after 1 p.m. I didn't ask him what it was all about, I knew he would tell me in his own good time – but I did have a pretty good idea.

In the next few weeks he became much more interested in Church, family prayers and everything Christian. He also made himself a wooden cross that he put on a chain around his neck. After a while I dared to ask him "Have you committed your life to Jesus?"

"Yes, Mum," he said, "when I was out walking that Monday."

That conversation was to be a great strength to me in the trials that followed.

Also that year I had my 5 days of heaven. I had always wanted to go to a Fountain Trust conference. Fountain Trust was an organization set up for the promotion of charismatic renewal in the Anglican Church. David was not very enthusiastic so I thought I would never get there. I read in Renewal Magazine that there was to be a five-day, midweek conference in Chester in July. (Renewal Magazine was at that time the Fountain Trust magazine but although Fountain Trust has now been wound up the magazine is still published – under the title Christianity and Renewal.)

Chester is only about 25 miles from Knutsford, so I thought and prayed about it. Then I talked it over with David to see if I might go on my own. The children would be at school all week and between them I thought the family would be capable of fending for themselves for 5 days – providing I left a well-stocked freezer!

David agreed, then I got cold feet, I hadn't been anywhere like this before on my own in my whole life. I had not left home until I married at 21 and then I'd had husband and family around me all the time. I was going to a strange place with a whole lot of people I didn't know, how would I cope?

I need not have worried, I arrived at Chester College, found my room and from the moment I got there I had the feeling of belonging to a family, and it was true, I was with part of the family of God. Many others had come on their own but we had all come with the one purpose in mind of drawing closer to God.

We had teaching seminars, times of praise and worship and in between we laughed and wept together and prayed for one another. Even as I sat quietly in the garden at coffee time on my own, God spoke to me. As I sat there in the sunshine I realized that I was sitting beside an empty, dry, ornamental pool with an inoperative fountain at the centre of it. The pool was badly cracked and broken. God showed me that this was a picture of his Church, broken, divided and dry. The fountain is symbolic of the Holy Spirit and God said he could not 'turn on' the Holy Spirit into a broken church; it would only be dissipated. The broken church needed repairing first. To repair the church we need to repent and forgive one another, and where this happens the Holy Spirit is poured out, and His power is not dissipated through cracks and divisions.

The climax to those five days was a Communion service in which we used the Anglican liturgy interspersed where possible and appropriate with free prayer and praise. It was the most beautiful time of worship and God's presence amongst us was almost tangible.

I arranged to give Freddy a lift home from the conference. We had only met at the conference but I already felt I knew him well and he lived quite near us in Wilmslow. Driving home we were having such a lovely time of fellowship and sharing in the car until we were halfway there. What made me think of it I don't know, but I suddenly realized I had left my Bible and notebooks behind. Fortunately, Freddy wasn't in too much of a hurry so we turned around and went back to Chester. We arrived there just as the Fountain Trust team were about to leave for London taking my Bible with them, God's perfect timing again. It just meant that Freddy and I had longer for fellowship. God took charge of every moment of that conference – even my forgetfulness!

Arriving home I found the family had survived my absence, even quite enjoying it, although the house looked rather a tip!

Five Days of Hell

> 'And we know that in all things God works for the good of those who love him who have been called according to his purpose.' Romans 8 verse 28. And 'Give thanks in all circumstances.' 1 Thessalonians 5 verse 18

Monday 21 January 1980 was just an ordinary Monday. I had spent the day in the usual routine of washing, cleaning the house after a family weekend and later trying to make something appetizing from the rather tiny remains of the Sunday joint. Monday was the only full day I had in the house as I was working at the bookshop the other 4 mornings, so

Mondays I did most of the housework. The first inkling I had that something was wrong was just after Sally came home from school at about 4.30 p.m. when the 'phone rang.

The woman's voice at the other end said, "Mrs Blanks?"

"Yes," I answered.

"We have your son Martin in Manchester Royal Infirmary casualty department, he has been hit by a bus," she said matter of factly.

"How serious is it?" I asked.

I can't remember now exactly what she said but she was very reassuring and I did not get the impression that he was badly hurt. Looking back now I suppose I was stupid to think that someone who has been hit by a bus would not be seriously hurt.

What should I do? My husband works in Manchester so I rang him.

"Martin's had an accident, he's been hit by a bus, they've taken him to Manchester Royal Infirmary."

"How bad is it?"

"I don't know, just get there as quick as you can and ring us when you know something."

Then I went and told Pop and Sally what had happened, but none of us could bear the thought of just waiting around for the phone to ring so we bundled into my car and drove to Manchester. I needed to be with my son.

We stopped at last at the hospital and I dashed up to the enquiry desk only to be told we had got the wrong hospital this was St Mary's Maternity Hospital and that M.R.I. was further up the road.

We finally parked the car and found our way to the Accident and Emergency department of M.R.I. where we found David and eventually saw Martin. We don't know if he knew we were there. When we managed to find the doctor the questions tumbled out. "What's wrong with him? Is he going to be alright? How did it happen?"

The doctor told us: "The main injuries are to his chest and lungs, though there are many lacerations and there could be more internal injuries."

"But is he going to be alright?" we asked again.

"He has to have an operation as soon as possible to remove the damaged lung and part of the other lung too," he replied.

"Will he be able to live with only part of a lung"?

The answer was a terse 'yes' and then he was gone.

Meanwhile, we were still trying to find out exactly how this accident had happened.

That evening passed in a blur, we telephoned family, who mostly live near London, and a few friends to ask them to pray. Our minister, Derek, came to be with us, and my friend Margaret Boler came too. Eventually, Margaret took Sally and Pop home while we waited at the hospital for news.

It was late in the evening when they operated on Martin. The thing I remember about that evening apart from the endless cups of tea was that at one point, Derek, David and I prayed together for Martin. The words, which continually pounded through my brain, were Romans 8 v 28 *'All things work together for good for those who love God.'* How could this be? Our only son desperately injured, fighting for life, how could I accept that this was working for anyone's good? I'd been learning this lesson, as I have already shared in this book, but that was on small things like broken sauce bottles and queues of traffic. But I knew that God was speaking to me there in that hospital waiting room. I shared this verse with Derek and David but how could we accept such a hard saying?

When eventually the operation was over and Martin was established on the ventilator and other equipment in intensive care, we were allowed to see him. It was frightening to walk into an intensive care unit and see a loved one attached to so much machinery. In Martin's case the ventilator was keeping him alive by breathing for him.

The surgeon told us that he had removed one lung and part of the other but assured us that Martin could live with just part of a lung, though he wouldn't be able to engage in sports. I didn't think this would worry him too much as, apart from lacrosse, coarse fishing was the main sport Martin enjoyed.

Having made certain that there was nothing more to be gained by staying on at the hospital we went out to my car to drive home, only to find that in my rush and anxiety I'd left the lights on and the battery was flat. Fortunately Derek was still with us and able to drive us home.

We needed to go home to try and sort things out but none of us could think very clearly and we had little sleep that night. We determined to make arrangements and return to the hospital as early as possible in the morning.

The telephone again brought us bad news, before we had time to complete our arrangements the hospital asked us to go as Martin's condition had worsened. That half hour drive to the hospital was a desolate time, neither of us spoke, lost in our own thoughts and prayers. Suddenly I felt I should take my authority as a Christian and banging my hand rather violently on the dashboard of the car I said, "Martin be healed in Jesus' name!"

On arrival at the hospital we were told "You have a very strong son," and that his condition was 'stablē'. This was a word that we would grow accustomed to hearing during those 5 days.

We spent the next nights and days at the hospital where we were given a room for the nights. The hospital staff were very kind. I don't think I have ever drunk so many cups of tea before, but it was one time in my life when I couldn't have cared less about food. We sat at Martins bedside hour after hour. We talked to him, sang choruses to him, prayed with him, prayed in tongues or just sat there quietly. He appeared to be unconscious and we had no idea how much he heard or understood, but somehow it was very important just to be there with him. We have since learned that though he could not communicate with us he probably heard much of what was said to him, as hearing is one of the last faculties to go.

As we sat there we did wonder what sort of life he could have after such a serious accident. On the other hand we know that God can and does heal – and we did have people from John O'Groats to Lands End praying for him, and God isn't deaf.

Sally in the meantime took charge at home. The telephone was a problem to Pop, as he was deaf in one ear. Sally found herself running the home and feeding the two of them in between answering numerous telephone calls and dealing with all the other enquiries. She was only fourteen but she coped so well.

When Saturday came we were utterly exhausted. We talked to the doctor and decided to go home that night to try and get some sleep. We left Martin wondering if we were doing the right thing, but we could be back in half an hour or so if necessary. Some time after midnight we were woken by the shrill sound of the telephone. The voice at the other end of the phone said, "Martin has taken a turn for the worse, please can you come back to the hospital?"

We later learned that he had been battling with pneumonia in the part of the lung he had left.

On the way to Manchester we were again silent, suddenly there was a voice, which seemed to be coming from the back seat of the car. David did not hear it, but it was so clear to me that I turned round to see who was speaking. There was no one there, it was then that I realized that it was God speaking. He said, "How much do you love Martin? Do you love him enough to let him go?"

I told David what had been said and in my heart all I could say was "I guess I'll have to." I do wish David had heard God speak too, but I knew God had spoken to me. When we arrived at the hospital, I was not surprised to be told that Martin was dead.

Naturally enough we wanted to see him and we had to wait while they got him ready. It was a nurse who I had not seen before who took us to see him. Her words to me were "You know, God tells us to give thanks in all circumstances" and later "God will give you the strength".

How did she know that giving thanks in all circumstances was a lesson that I was learning? It was a pretty daring thing to say to a newly bereaved mother. I suspect she was an angel in disguise.

It was good to see Martin without all the tubes and machinery but as we looked at him there, we knew that **he** wasn't actually there. I can't explain it but the essential Martin was gone, looking back now I regret not touching him, but at the time there seemed to be no need as **he** wasn't there.

Then began the difficult job of telling everyone the news, my parents and our brothers and sisters living so far away hadn't seen Martin, just receiving daily bulletins, so they were very shocked. Sally had been convinced that Martin would get well, how would she cope with it? Pop had suffered several tragedies in his life, how would he come to terms with this latest blow?

Later that day the doctor came and gave me a sedative so that I might get some much-needed sleep.

When my sister-in-law, Joan, heard the news she came to stay and was a great strength to us during the days leading up to the funeral. One day

I had gone to the toilet when the pain of Martin's death hit me so hard it was like a physical pain and I howled with grief. It was Joan who came to find me and hugged me tight.

The love, concern and practical help that had been poured upon us by our friends from the church, our neighbours, and so many people, had already overwhelmed us. Now the help and loving care came like an avalanche. Cards, letters, flowers and practical gifts like cakes and even complete meals, poured in.

David arranged for the funeral on Friday 1 February with a service in our own church followed by a short one at the crematorium. Our neighbours kindly took over the responsibility of catering for that occasion. We needed something substantial because of the distance many would be travelling. Victor, the minister who had married us and baptized Martin was coming to share in the services.

The next five days passed for us as if in a dream, or probably more realistically a nightmare. Anyone who has experienced bereavement will recognize how we felt. Each day we would wake and then it seemed like a black cloud would descend as we remembered our loss. Each day you need courage just to get out of bed and face another day. Day after day the postman brought more letters and cards of condolence. As soon as the mail came I would sit and open each letter or card, knowing that each would make me cry. Despite this daily weep I needed to <u>know</u> that others cared. So many people wanted to give us flowers that we set up a memorial fund for Martin, which reached over £400. and was divided between our Church Youth Club and Manchester Royal Infirmary.

Each of the members of the immediate family reacted differently to bereavement; Sally missed him very much (and still does) he had always been there for her. She has been known to remark that we are not a 'proper' family now. Though she was only fourteen she showed great courage and was a great help to us. David was (and still is) heartbroken, he still finds it difficult to talk about Martin. I remember our next-door neighbours remarking months later that he must be getting over it as they could hear him singing again. He always has sung lustily around the house. Pop went quieter than usual but showed little of his grief. My own parents were heartbroken, having brought up three daughters, their first grandson Martin was special and now he was gone. Dad – not one to show his feelings, was desolate. Grandchildren don't die before grandparents, do they?

The day of the funeral dawned bright and sunny with clear blue skies but bitterly cold. Our church was full; many of Martin's school friends and teachers were there. There were local friends of all the family and relations. I don't remember a lot about the service itself except that one hymn was 'God is love let heaven adore him' and one of the readings included Romans 8 v 28. *'All things work together for good to those that love God.'*

I kept fairly calm and quiet that day but the grief hit me hard on the following day – Saturday – I just couldn't stop crying. Mum in desperation suggested we went for a walk, thinking that if we went out I would have to stop crying, but even as I walked up the road the tears continued to roll down my cheeks. The grief has to come some time.

Martin

> *'Jesus knowing their thoughts took a little child and made him stand beside him. Then he said to them "Whoever welcomes this little child in my name welcomes me; and whoever welcomes me welcomes the one who sent me. For he who is the least among you all – he is the greatest"'*

Luke 6 verse 47 and 48

Our firstborn came into our lives on 10th May 1963. He was 7lb 13 oz. And had tight brown curls flattened to his head, with blue eyes. He soon lost his baby hair, which was replaced with blond hair, which darkened as he grew up. He smiled freely and developed an infectious laugh. He was barely 3 months old when he first chuckled out loud. Pop was with us when it happened otherwise I might have been tempted to think I'd imagined it – it was such a grown up chuckle.

We took him away on his first holiday when he was 15 months old to Broadstairs with David's brother, Cliff and his wife Joan. What could be more natural than setting a young child down on the sand? Unfortunately, Martin thought the sand so delicious that he ate it handful by handful, which had dire consequences on the number and state of dirty nappies he produced. To stop him reaching the sand Pop bought a small blue and yellow blow-up paddling pool and we sat him in that. He couldn't reach the sand from there.

One of Mum's treasured memories of Martin was when, at 2 and 3 years old, he would say. "Please Nanny, Martin help you?" – this was with anything from cleaning out the grate to washing up.

He was a sensitive, soft hearted boy and quite nervous. He had a problem with protruding top front teeth because he'd sucked his thumb as a baby. He was teased and bullied at school about this. Towards the end of his time in junior school he slipped on the school floor, fell and broke his two front teeth. The dentist managed to save them but it was some time before they were capped and the treatment started to straighten them, which made him even more the butt of jokes and teasing.

One lovely memory is of the 'bundles' David and the children had. 'Bundles' happened when the children and their Dad were larking about together and getting a bit boisterous then one or other of them would shout 'bundle' and they would end up in a writhing, tickling, mass on the rug in the hall – even the dog used to join in! I would look on wondering when one of them would get hurt, or disappear out of the way so that I could not worry about it.

When he was nine he went on a school trip to Paris and was away for a week. We missed him dreadfully as it was the longest time he'd been away from us and we had no news of him until he got back. I went to the school to pick him up after the trip and parked the car a little way from the school gates. I could see him talking to his friends. As I looked I thought there was something wrong with his legs, they looked distinctly mottled, as I got closer I could see the mottling was dirt!

When we got home I said, "Whatever's happened to your legs, they're mottled with dirt, didn't they have showers in Paris?"

"Course they did Mum," he replied, " but they were unisex showers, I couldn't go in there with all the girls, could I?"

When they were little, both the children enjoyed a bedtime story and David usually got the job. He read to them a lot but they always wanted to hear a 'Pongo the mouse story'. David invented a family of mice. Pongo was father, Millie was mother and the children were Eeny, Meeny, Miny and Mo. David always made the stories topical and I wish now I'd tape-recorded them. After the story came prayers and "goodnight, God bless"

As many children do, both ours had trouble saying 'th' it would usually turn into 'f', and to encourage them to say it properly David got them to repeat the phrase "I think saving three and threepence is thrifty." It soon did the trick.

In Knutsford on the Saturday nearest to May Day there is a procession with a May Queen, a whole day of celebrations and a fair on the Heath. One year, when we took the children to the fair, they went on the bouncy castle. Shoes were abandoned at the entrance and off they bounced. It was quite a cold day and Martin had on his duffle coat. When their time was up we found that Martin had bounced so energetically that every single button had come off his coat and were lost forever.

When we watched any exciting or frightening programmes like Dr Who and the Daleks on television Martin would hide behind the settee hopping up and down in excitement and fear, peeping out at intervals to see what was happening. He always wanted to watch but how much he actually saw, I'm not sure.

Martin could always amuse himself and played happily on his own with Lego or models or designing a new spaceship. On the other hand, Sally always wanted company, even if it was her brother or mum.

As he grew older he enjoyed making plastic models of aeroplanes and other militaria. He spent hours gluing and painting them. Saturday morning was pocket money day and Martin spent it choosing the latest model. He was always broke after Saturday whereas Sally always managed to hang on to some of her pocket money. Once the models were finished they would be hung from his bedroom ceiling.

He had quite a difficult start at school so that when it came to time for him to prepare to change schools at 11 we just assumed that he would go to the local comprehensive school. His teacher, however, had other ideas and suggested that he take the entrance exam for one of the Manchester direct grant schools. He took the one for William Hulme Grammar School and did well enough to gain himself a free place. The year before he died he had gained good grades in GCE O levels and had started his A level course in Chemistry, Maths and Physics. His father hoped that he would eventually go to university, although Martin was not keen to leave home. He was a home loving boy. David and Martin used to leave home together during those years to travel to Manchester – at least as far as the station.

He loved science fiction books and films. At school both the children were shown a film about the dangers of smoking. Pop had smoked since he was in his teens because he had worked as a cigarette machine operator, which meant he had an allowance of cigarettes until he retired, and David too had taken it up when there was a free supply available at home. The children begged their Dad and Grandad to stop smoking – David did, but it took a severe bout of bronchitis, when he was in his seventies, to stop Pop. The children were heartbroken when their entreaties didn't stop him there and then, they loved their Grandad deeply.

Martin was not a very popular lad because he was shy and found relationships difficult. He also had acne as he reached puberty, which didn't help his confidence. He had one good friend locally, Ian Turner, and they would go off coarse fishing together. We parents took it in turns to take them to the latest favourite fishing ground. Our neighbour, Verlie, remembers one particular fishing trip when it was very cold, Martin confided that he had his pyjamas on under his trousers as an extra layer! This was something I did not know until much later.

He had one or two friends at school but because they lived a long way away he did not invite them home so we didn't get to know them.

During the last year of his life, since he'd become a Christian, he seemed to us to be opening out, becoming more confident and more accepted. There was one girl at the church whom he was very keen on, but he hadn't got as far as asking her out.

In that same year, when he was fifteen and Sally thirteen, we went on a camping holiday in France. The first site we stayed on was in the Dordogne, a beautiful area near prehistoric caves and the town of Sarlat. This site had many facilities including a swimming pool, which we loved. The only trouble was that we had uninvited guests in our tent – lizards, I suppose it could have been worse, it could have been snakes, which I loathe.

The other site was on the Atlantic coast at Royan, set on sand dunes close to the sea. This was an area noted for its nudist beaches. We, being British, were a bit surprised to see families playing beach cricket in the raw! Martin took to going for long walks on his own down the beach, broadening his education.

In 1976 we bought a beagle puppy and called him Skipper. This was a very appropriate name because from the moment he entered the house he became boss. This was our first dog and we were all a bit frightened of him when we first brought him home. He seemed to be all sharp claws, sharp teeth and just everywhere causing havoc or puddles! As he settled in and became quieter we grew to love him. Martin, in particular, would often sit on the floor hugging him when human relationships became too difficult.

While Skipper was a pup David encouraged him to sit on his lap, and then when David had a serious operation on his back and had to lay on the settee the dog slept beside him. It became such a habit that whenever David sat down the dog thought it was his right to use him as a dog basket and would clamber aboard unasked. As soon as David came home he would have to change into his oldest clothes.

Two years before he died Martin had a mysterious illness, which made one of his eyes swell and bulge out of his head, and he ran a high temperature. He was treated with antibiotics but was very ill for a few days. We took him to see a specialist and his head was X-rayed and we discovered that he had no sinus on that side of his head. The final diagnosis was cellulitis. It affected his sight and it took some time for his eye to get back to normal.

Martin had learned to play the piano but became despondent after he failed his first exam by just a few marks. We hoped that he would take it up again in the future.

Perhaps my favourite memory in that last year is of Martin coming home from school, by this time he was over 6 feet tall. He would come in, give me a hug, and say "Hallo, little Mum."

The Holy Spirit the Comforter?

'Out of the depths I cry to you O Lord.' Psalm 130 verse 1

The accident, which led to Martin's death, was still very much a mystery to us but the police were investigating it. They indicated that there could be a prosecution of some of the lads who had been involved. Of course we wanted to know how he died but the question of whether someone was prosecuted for it was not something we thought a lot about. Coming to terms with his death was enough to cope with. He was no longer a part of our lives, whatever had caused it, he was dead. I was thankful to know he was a Christian and know we will meet again one day, as I believe he is in heaven with his Lord.

The day after the funeral I was due to take part in a performance of 'The Witness', which was being put on in the Civic Hall in Knutsford. I went along in the afternoon to listen to the practice as I have always found the music encouraging and felt God's presence in the singing. My Christian friends in the choir were very supportive and caring.

As I sat there I found myself singing along and decided I wanted to take part in the evening. I don't remember much about the performance but at the end I was asked to give my testimony. Much to my surprise I felt able to speak and spoke about the reassurance that I have that Martin is in heaven. I can only say that the Holy Spirit gave me the strength, I had none of my own. Sharing in such a way exhausted me. I look back now and wonder how I managed to do it but I suppose it was because I was still in the numbness of shock – at times it seemed as though it had all happened to someone else.

For a long time after Martin's death, when I woke in the morning for a few seconds I'd be all right, then the realization of my loss would come and descend like a cloud of blackness. There were a few days when I was certain of God giving me strength but there were many others when I seemed to be struggling on my own. I felt like a drowning woman gasping for breath to keep alive for just a few more seconds. Doing ordinary things seemed to take all my energy and strength and anything extra was out of the question. Even though I was exhausted by the end of the day I found it difficult to sleep and I had to have some pills to help. I felt guilty about this, I was a Christian and I should be able to cope, shouldn't I?

Many questions went through my mind. Shouldn't the Holy Spirit be comforting me? What is comfort anyway? I had always thought of comfort as taking away the pain. I had thought that if I were bereaved the Holy Spirit would take away the pain. I began to realize that the only way the pain would go was if Martin came back to life again and that wasn't going to happen. I looked up the word 'comfort' in the dictionary to find that its original meaning was strengthen. The

Comforter is the strengthener.

Coming to terms with this tragedy we needed strength and courage and this is what we got from the Holy Spirit. It was rather like when I was giving birth to Sally at home. I had a very long and painful labour because of the way she was positioned. In desperation I said to my neighbour (herself the mother of three) "I can't bear it".

Her reply was a speedy, "You'll have to!" – not very sympathetic but true! Somehow with God's help we <u>would</u> live on and bear our loss.

A fortnight after the funeral my parents decided that it was time for them to go home. I didn't want them to go, but they felt they must. It was a Wednesday quite early in the morning when I drove them to Wilmslow to catch the London train. That day after they had gone seemed endless. In desperation I turned the radio on some time after 4 p.m. just to hear someone's voice and try to shut out my thoughts. I needed something to dig me out of the mire of pain and self-pity. The first words to come from the speaker were Romans 8 v 28. *'And we know that in all things God works for the good of those who love him who have been called according to his purpose,'* I found that I had tuned in to Choral Evensong. Here was that verse again but I still could not see how what had happened could work together for good for anyone least of all me. I wanted my lovely son Martin!

During this terrible time Pop was always a listening ear and I would often talk to him, but he had his own grief to come to terms with and I did not want to heap more on to him.

My prayer has always been (in my better moments) that God <u>will</u> work this tragedy for good, for the good of as many people as possible. If it had to happen at all, then it shouldn't be wasted, but redemptive. One thing, which I did see very quickly, was some reconciliation. I was one of the people who in the early 1970s had been filled with the Holy Spirit and we had been treated with suspicion, fear and antagonism – much of this disappeared, they realized we were still human; when we are cut we bleed. The love, which was already there blossomed and we received much practical help, prayer and visits. I appreciated the cooking that people did for us, as cooking for me at that time took such an effort and, because I wasn't hungry, sometimes I couldn't be bothered at all.

We had flowers at home fit to grace a florist's shop for several months.

I particularly remember a magnificent bouquet, which arrived in May, a very appropriate time because it was Martin's birthday month and the inquest was held in May. They came from a lady who I had first met through the healing services we held for a year. Her daughter had been healed through them and the whole family had become Christians. She remembered her own bereavement – her husband had died 2 or 3 years before – and how the pain had been greater after a few months than at the beginning. The reality that you will never see or touch or hear that person again has kicked in; you realize that your life has gone on without them being a part of it. This feels like a daily loss. She wanted me to know that she knew how I would be feeling; I was very touched by her thoughtfulness.

Going to church was difficult. We wanted to go but at times, particularly during the hymns we would find ourselves in tears. We have grown up in this country hiding our grief away – the British stiff upper lip. At this time we just couldn't help crying, we either had to accept ourselves as we were and cry during the hymns, or stay away from Church. We decided to stick it out and go to church.

I found people's reactions after Martin's death varied enormously. Some gave me a hug, others expressed sympathy, others did not mention Martin at all and some avoided me altogether – actually crossing the road when they saw me coming. I can understand all these reactions because if you haven't experienced such a tragedy yourself you are tongue-tied. I remembered how I had been with the family at Broxbourne who lost a son in an accident. On the other hand if you have experienced bereavement then you can be afraid of showing your feelings. I found the people who helped the most were those who prayed for me or with me, gave me a hug, held my hand or wept with me.

All through our grief we found our dog to be a great help. Whatever we felt like, Skipper still needed feeding and walking. He did not show grief, he was a constant loving factor. He didn't make emotional demands upon us. We could fondle him and make a fuss of him without complications. He, like us, did not forget Martin, however, as we discovered when, some months after Martin's death, Pop put on Martin's parka to go out into the garden, the dog went wild with excitement. Martin's smell was obviously still on the coat; needless to say, we wept at that realization.

As we were adjusting to Martin's death we found that we did not cry all the time (not even I could cry all the time) but the grief within us built up to a kind of tension that finally exploded into a row, which eventually ended in tears. Once the tears came the tension broke. At first this happened quite frequently but gradually the time between lengthened. As the time lengthened, it became more difficult to recognize exactly what was happening, so the tension without the release of tears, was sometimes not recognized as grief and caused problems with relationships in the family.

One thing, which surprised me about grief, was the very physical nature of it. It hits you in the stomach; it is utterly exhausting and affects every part of you. People talk about heartache – stomach ache was much more our experience. For the first few weeks it was like living in a nightmare. Only after about two months did the reality of the fact that we would never see Martin again in this life hit me and then the pain seemed unbearable. I was thankful for the distraction of the part-time job I had in the bookshop where my workmates were very kind and understanding.

I had difficulty getting down to housework (even more than usual) in fact, I found it difficult to stay at home at all, as home seemed too empty and full of memories. One friend, Sylvia, who had been through bereavement herself, gave me some advice, which I found helpful.

She said, "If you don't want to stay at home, don't. Get out and be with other people. The time will come when you will be able to stay at home again."

I took her advice and found over the months that she was right.

One reaction, which I found hard to understand, was when well meaning Christians said I could be healed of the grief for Martin's death. This made me feel guilty, for the pain I felt (and still feel from time to time) is very real. My love for my firstborn is very real and the pain of loss is very real. Are they saying that God can take that pain away? Was God's pain taken away when His son died? Or is that pain part of the cost of loving? I could not blame them for feeling like this as I had a similar idea about the comfort of the Holy Spirit before I experienced bereavement.

They talked about this as 'inner healing'. What I have read about inner healing it seems to be a matter of recognizing wrongs done to us in the past, or ways we have wronged others, and forgiving and being forgiven.

I find God does this continually in my life. I looked at my attitude to Martin's death and I did go through times of being angry with God, which is a fairly normal reaction when you believe God to be all power-ful. I always tried to be honest with Him and I believe He understood me and forgave me. The Psalms gave me a lead in this – some of their sentiments are very powerful like the one at the start of this chapter. By God's grace we didn't want vengeance on the boys involved in Martin's death. I could not see what I needed healing from. My experience of grief is that it is a natural, painful, process, which you have to go through to be healed from. I think of it rather like a deep physical wound which has to heal from the inside out.

Some time before Martin's death, I was asked to take the chair at Eastbrook Hall's afternoon anniversary meeting in Bradford on 18 March. Early in March I was asked "Do you feel able to take part after all that has happened to you?"

My reply was, "I will be all right as long as you don't mention Martin".

God, however, had other ideas as, when I was preparing the Chairman's remarks I felt I should share something of what had hap-pened to us in the last 2 months. Again, I can only give God the glory; He gave me the strength and the words to say. I took two friends with me as company on the drive and we were all three blessed. The blessing was there but the exhaustion followed.

We had to wait until May before the inquest into Martin's death was held. Friends, out of concern for me, suggested that I should not go to the inquest but I knew I had to be there. I wanted to know as much as possible about what had caused my only son's death. I had brought him into the world; I wanted to see him through to the end.

The story that unfolded was that there was rivalry between boys from Martins school and the local comprehensive. The day of Martin's acci-dent boys from the comprehensive had decided it was the day to 'get' boys from William Hulme. Martin, who always got away from school quickly in order to catch his train home, was the first to get to the bus stop. A boy from the comprehensive, encouraged by friends, had gone up to punch him. Whether he had succeeded or Martin had stepped in front of the bus whilst trying to dodge out of the way we don't know, but no case was brought against the lads. The police were very apologetic that they could not get enough evidence to bring a case against them.

At the inquest, we saw the boys involved but neither David nor I felt anger nor wanted revenge; that must surely have been God's grace.

After we got home that day we had a visit from a national newspaper reporter. What she asked was, "What are you going to do now?" and "Don't you want justice?" What she really meant was, weren't we going to seek revenge. The interview was never published as we wanted to forgive and forget and that isn't newsworthy.

We do sometimes wonder if the boy who punched Martin ever thinks of what he did and what affect it has had upon his life. We have prayed that it will bring him and the other boys involved to know the Lord.

The evening of the day of the inquest we had our regular prayer meeting and I went along as usual. My friends wanted to know what had happened and having told them I burst into floods of tears and could not be consoled. I couldn't stay on to the meeting but went home to an early night.

Some time after the first Easter after Martin had died a minister friend said, "You must have found Easter encouraging this year."

I did not have the chance to answer him but would have said, "No I didn't". In truth I'd found Easter a trial. What I wanted was the physical presence of my son; I wanted to see him, speak to him and hug him! Why couldn't God raise my son to life? My head rationalized, but that is what my heart wanted more than anything!

After the funeral there was something which worried me and which I did not share with anyone but the Lord. David, out of concern for me, had made all the funeral arrangements and I didn't want to upset him by sharing my feelings. The problem I had was that I had been horrified at the thought of Martin being cremated. I knew HE was not really there but still the thought of burning bothered me. About 6 months after his death I had a dream and in my dream Martin had had an accident but this time he had been burned. David advised me not to go to see him, but the nurse said to come. Inside the hospital, a nurse called me to go and see Martin. I went down the corridor and there he stood smiling at me and perfectly whole. He did not speak, just smiled at me; and then I woke up. This dream seemed to me to be a message from God, which set my mind at rest about the cremation. I knew Martin was okay.

CHAPTER SIX

Trying to Resume a Normal Life

Aglow

'Be aglow and burning with the Spirit.' Romans 12 verse 11
(Amplified Bible.)

After Martin's death as I faced bereavement I had terrible moments and even days of desperation when I shouted at God and asked him "WHY?" But as everyone tells you life does go on. I found one of the most difficult things to take was that now life was to go on without Martin – he was in the past. We had to plan our life without him. I remember shouting one day "But Lord I want my son!" It was soon after this outburst that I had a very clear promise that I would have "many sons". I can't remember now how the promise came but it was very clear and stayed with me. I did not expect, nor want, a literal fulfilment of this promise but I did somehow feel that God would fill the empty space left by Martin's death.

It was soon after this promise that I went with Margaret Boler to an Aglow meeting at Bowdon and was asked by another friend, on the spur of the moment, to give my testimony. Although I was still raw after Martin's death God once more gave me the courage and strength to speak without dissolving into floods of tears. These testimonies always left me exhausted but encouraged – God really was with me giving me strength and courage.

That was my first experience of Women's Aglow Fellowship, which takes its name from the text at the start of this chapter. It is an organization, which started in America for outreach among women. It is rather like a women's version of Full Gospel Business Men's Fellowship International. The women form chapters and hold meetings in hotels or community centres where they share a meal, praise and worship, and then one or two women give their testimonies. The idea is to invite non-

Christian friends so that through the testimonies they will learn something of the relevance of belief in God for today. At the end of the meeting an opportunity is given for commitment, prayer and counselling.

Women in Knutsford became so enthusiastic about Aglow that a meeting was held in my home to see about the possibility of starting a chapter. It seemed a good idea to me but was it something the Lord wanted me personally to be involved in?

We went to a weekend conference to find out more about Aglow and it was there in the last meeting that I got my answer. A woman read the story of Jesus on the cross from John chapter 19, verse 26 says '*Jesus saw His mother and the disciple He loved standing there and so he said to his mother "Woman here is your son".*' I took this as a message from God to me, the first of my 'many sons' was to be 'Aglow'. Others were to follow.

What is so exciting about Aglow is that it gives an opportunity to spread the Gospel among women who would probably never go near a church but would enjoy a meal out with friends. At these meetings married women, single women, divorcees and widows can meet together on equal terms and not feel the odd one out. With no denominational tag, it attracted women from all denominations and none. We found it a great blessing in Knutsford although it didn't grow as much as we had hoped.

It was in and through Aglow that I experienced more of the operation of the gifts of the Holy Spirit.

During the worship times we would often sing in tongues and there would be speaking in tongues with interpretation. A woman who was weeping gave one message we received in this way. This was that message:

"I really live in you and yet you weep and yet you fear and yet you tremble. I really live in you, I am part of your life, everything you do, I do. Everything you strive for, I strive for, and yet you so often will not let my power flow through you. So often you are not aware of my guiding hand, so often you think your own thoughts and look at your own strength, and you do not listen to the thoughts or lean on the strength of the Lord your God. Come unto me. Open yourself up to me this morning that I might truly live in you. Cast aside your own strength, cast aside your own belief, cast aside your own concerns and just rest in me and together we will walk through life. Together we will walk to the Royal Kingdom; together we will climb those

mountains and cross those raging streams. Yes, they are before you, but I am with you."

At the end of the meetings, when the opportunity was given for anyone who needed prayer, to come forward, they came to receive Jesus as their Saviour and Lord, to be baptized in the Holy Spirit, for healing or, sometimes, for other problems. We soon learnt that we had to deal with any occult involvement first of all, as this would be a blockage to blessing from God. Things like involvement in Yoga, Spiritualism, ouija board, horoscopes, the cult of U.F.Os to name but a few, had to be renounced and repented of. Sometimes when we omitted this procedure we would get a 'word of knowledge' which would guide us. The word of knowledge is a gift of the Holy Spirit; it is a piece of information about a person or situation which you had no means of knowing except by God revealing it to you – like the word 'earthquake' I had before Bob went to Japan, mentioned earlier.

Most of the women we counselled in these meetings were totally unknown to us so we had to rely on the Holy Spirit to guide us with words of knowledge and words of wisdom. Whilst praying for one woman for healing of high blood pressure, as I closed my eyes I had a mind picture of an angry woman. When I told her about my picture she admitted that she was angry with her neighbour. Once that was revealed to her she knew she had to repent of her anger and forgive her neighbour – only then could we pray successfully for her healing.

On another occasion whilst praying for healing the word resentment came into my mind – which was shared with the woman I was praying for. She admitted this, repented, gave up her resentment and we went on to pray for her healing. These were quite common experiences in our ministry in Aglow.

We often experienced the gifts of the Holy Spirit in our prayer meetings where we prayed for the work of Aglow. Two incidents come to mind when we were praying for members or friends. A woman whose husband was out of work asked us: "Please will you pray for my husband, that he will get the right job he has two interviews arranged but I want him to get the right job, not just any job?"

As we prayed the word 'pie' came into my mind. On sharing this with the group the woman said, "One of the jobs he has applied for is one with a company which makes cakes and pies." He got the job.

One evening Margaret Boler said "Will you pray for my neighbour she's expecting her fourth child and she's had trouble delivering the other three?"

As we prayed I had a mind picture of a baby being born naturally. When I shared this with the others I was told, "If that happens it will be a miracle, the other three were born by Caesarean Section." – something I had not known. The miracle happened, her fourth child was born naturally. Praise the Lord!

I find that God speaks to me sometimes through dreams; I had heard through the grapevine that a yoga group wanted to use a room on our church premises for their exercise sessions – and I was concerned. My concern about Yoga stems from the fact that each of the Yoga positions is dedicated to a particular Hindu God and this is not a good thing for Christians to be involved in. Early one morning I had a dream and in my dream I saw a very large, strong spider's web, but the spider was not immediately obvious. As I looked again I shuddered as I saw that the large spider (not my favourite creature) was there, but was hiding, as they often do, right in the corner of the web. I felt God said that this was like yoga – looking innocent but being a trap nevertheless. I shared this with our minister, I don't know if my dream influenced him or not but the yoga group was not allowed on our premises.

That same year I was desperately in need of healing myself. I had a problem with my gall bladder, which had persisted for fifteen years. I would have bouts of (sometimes agonizing) pain and nausea. I had been X-rayed twice, but nothing abnormal showed up, not even a gallstone. Nevertheless, the doctor thought it was gall bladder trouble. I ate as little fat as possible but I was at the end of my tether. I decided to follow the injunction in James chapter 5 and verse 14 where it says, '*Is any one of you sick? He should call the elders of the church to pray over him and anoint him with oil in the name of the Lord. And the prayer offered in faith will make the sick person well; the Lord will raise him up. If he has sinned he will be forgiven.*' Our Minister Graham Evans came to our weekly Bible Study group and he prayed with me there.

I had already made an appointment to see a specialist that week under our private health scheme, but that oil certainly got things moving, within a week I had seen the specialist and was in hospital having a badly diseased gall bladder removed.

I was in a private hospital with my own room for this operation and I felt lonely and isolated, particularly the night before the operation. I wish I could say I felt God's presence with me but in spite of the fact that lots of people were praying, all I felt was fear. It did not help when the following day after the operation I woke up with a drip in my arm and a tube in my stomach. I didn't know that this was normal procedure, I thought something had gone drastically wrong. No one had thought to tell me what to expect.

What did encourage me, was that as I began to feel better, and was able to walk around the hospital, I talked to some of the other patients. There were two women in particular who were wealthy and would not normally move in the same circles as me. Their main concerns seemed to be keeping themselves looking young and beautiful. I talked to them about Jesus being my friend. One of them was suffering from cancer and I got the impression that she was used to spending money to sort out her problems but this problem would not be solved by money – there was nothing the doctors could do, the cancer was inoperable. I did visit her at home and pray with her for healing. We had long talks and I hope that by the time she died Jesus was her friend too. It was a great privilege and made me realize that, even if I didn't FEEL Him with me, He was there all the same.

If God had given me the choice I would have had Him heal me with a touch; but He decided it would be by the surgeon's knife, otherwise I would not have met those women.

I was Vice President of Knutsford Aglow from March 1981 until September 1983 when I felt I should step down from the position. In that time we saw many women become Christians, others baptized in the Holy Spirit and others healed. We listened to many moving and challenging testimonies and enjoyed deep fellowship with the Lord and one another. I give thanks to God for the experience I had in counselling and the gifts of the Holy Spirit through Aglow.

I do sometimes go to Aglow meetings but God has drawn me back more into my own church situation to work now.

Journey of a lifetime

'O Jerusalem, Jerusalem, you who kill the prophets and stone those sent to you, how often I have longed to gather your children together, as a hen gathers her chicks under her wings, but you were not willing.' Matthew 8 verse 37

Experiencing the death of a loved one suddenly, as we had, makes you realize the uncertainty of life. Who can say we have tomorrow? So for a while at least we found ourselves jolted into action. To see the land where Jesus had lived, died and been resurrected was a lifetime dream for both of us, so we planned a holiday to Israel. Sally did not want to come as she was planning a holiday later with her friend Lisa. I was anxious about this as, having lost Martin, I hardly wanted to let Sally out of my sight. However, she was old enough to make her own decision and she would stay with Pop.

We only booked in January to go at Easter, which fell at the end of March that year. It would be an extra blessing to be there at Easter and we hoped it would be cooler then.

It was the Wednesday before Easter when we checked into Heathrow for the El Al Boeing 747 flight for Tel Aviv. After thorough checking of our baggage for bombs or weapons, we were allowed to board this massive plane. Once the passengers were on board I had serious doubts about it even getting off the ground, let alone flying us to Tel Aviv! As it was, touchdown was a bit frightening as the vibration was so bad that many of the overhead baggage lockers flew open.

Passover and Easter coincided that year, as they had that first Easter nearly 2,000 years ago, so half the plane was filled with tourists, the other half with Jews returning for the Passover. Our meal on the plane was accompanied by Matzos (unleavened bread) not very appetizing rather like water biscuits. It is still every Jew's ambition to spend Passover in Jerusalem and as we approached Tel Aviv they sang and cheered.

As we stepped off the plane it seemed that we had entered a different world. The warmth hit us, and David said. "It even smells different, – sort of warm and scented."

From Tel Aviv we went by coach to Jerusalem where we stayed for the first part of our visit. About 7 a.m. the following day we began exploring Jerusalem the golden – it really is golden, built as it is, mostly of honey gold stone. It is hard to imagine that a city fought over for so many thousands of years could feel 'holy' but that is what I felt as we walked around.

Jerusalem is a city of contrasts, rich and poor, European and Arabic dress and everywhere the orthodox Jews in their traditional clothes, dark suits, black hats and the curls of hair in front of their ears. Even young boys had these, which looked strange to us. All the Jewish men, if they had not the black hats and curls, wore the little skull-caps. Here, modern life, and life as it has been for centuries, exist side by side. Transport from Mercedes taxis, coaches and other motor vehicles zoomed around the city in between heavily laden donkeys threading their way through the narrow streets. We even saw the occasional camel. All the motor vehicles were driven one way – dangerously! Drivers put their foot down on the accelerator, their finger on the horn and away!

I don't think trading can have changed in centuries. On the streets of the old city small shops, often appearing more like caves, tumbled their wares on to the busy pavements. Here were coffee shops selling, hot, strong Turkish coffee and other shops selling exotic cakes and sweetmeats, others selling souvenirs, household goods and clothes. Then there were people with carts selling food on street corners.

You could buy almost anything from the shops in old Jerusalem, but you had to bargain for everything. You never paid the advertised price but haggled to get the best deal possible. Being British it came hard to us but we soon found that we could get really 'stung' if we didn't haggle. After a while we became proud of the hard bargains we had driven, and boasted to one another of the latest best buy. Soft, loose Indian style dresses were fashionable at the time and I bought one for Sally and one for myself for a song – my favourite bargains from the trip.

In the first few days we went to the Church of the Paternoster, on the traditional site where Jesus taught the Lord's Prayer. This one prayer unites every denomination of the church and is painted up in and on the Church in many languages, the most well known prayer in the world so simple, yet so profound.

The garden of Gethsemane, the Mount of Olives and the Church of Dominus Flevit (the Lord wept) were next on our itinerary. The Mount of Olives was the vantage point from which Jesus looked across Jerusalem and wept over it. With its current tensions and troubles I'm sure He still weeps.

The Garden of Gethsemane was where Jesus went on the night of his betrayal and his disciples couldn't even keep awake with him. Then Judas came and betrayed Him to the authorities with a kiss. The olive trees we saw there could well have been the ones that were there in Jesus day as it is very difficult to kill them. Even if an olive tree is cut down or burnt the root remains and the tree re-grows. Their trunks can be grotesque in shape but are topped by fine, grey green foliage. Olive wood is very hard and is used to make many souvenirs.

We visited the church of St Peter in Gallicantu (Caiaphas' House). We saw there the entrance hole to the dungeon, where Jesus probably spent the last night before the Crucifixion. I had never considered before where he had spent that night. This dungeon was just a hole in the rock that would have been, dark, dank and cold. There were no stairs down; the only way in was to be physically dropped down into it.

We took a coach to Hebron and the Mosque of Abraham. This is the traditional burial place of Abraham and a shrine of interest to Moslems, Jews and Christians, which is guarded by armed soldiers. I felt very intimidated as these soldiers body searched us before we were allowed inside.

During our stay in Israel we became used to seeing armed soldiers about. They seemed almost casual at times, resting on the grass with their guns beside them. We were saddened by the number of young children begging and took care to avoid the many pickpockets in operation everywhere.

We visited Bethlehem and the Church of the Nativity, which seemed rather too ornate to be connected with the bare stable of the Bible story of Jesus birth – but it did seem appropriate, that as we approached the manger area we had to bend down to get inside.

On Good Friday we were up early and followed on foot the via Dolorosa (the way of the cross) past the pool of Bethesda, where the cripple was healed, to the Upper Room where the Last Supper was celebrated, and then on to the Church of the Holy Sepulchre. Again this is a very ornate church, which it is hard to associate with the original sepulchre.

On we walked to the Temple Mount and the Western Wall, usually known as the Wailing Wall. This is the one section of the wall of the temple, which is left standing. Many Jews go there to pray and perform ceremonies and the continual prayer sounds like wailing.

There is a small section where women are allowed to go and pray, and I went, full of awe, to join my prayers with the millions down the centuries. Many women had stuffed their written prayer requests into cracks in the wall. The presence of God seemed to 'crackle' in the air at the Wailing Wall.

We walked on through the Damascus gate, out of the old city of Jerusalem and into the Garden Tomb. This is a cave set in gardens, which was used as a sepulchre. It was only discovered quite recently, and it is suggested that this was the tomb where Jesus was laid. Historians say that the Church of the Holy Sepulchre is the more likely site for the tomb but I found the Garden tomb, because of its simplicity, much more as I imagined Jesus tomb to be. At my first visit I sat quietly there absorbing the peace and tranquillity. It was moving (though rather cold) to go there at 6 a.m. on Easter Sunday morning for an English Language service to celebrate the resurrection. There were several services in different languages that Easter morning.

A trip by coach took us to the Dead Sea and Massada. This journey took us through the Judean wilderness, where the land, which is called desert, is not sandy, (as I had expected) but rocky, stony, dusty and very bleak. This is where Jesus is thought to have spent his 40 days and nights in the wilderness when He was tempted by the devil. There were many loaf-sized stones around that the devil could have tempted him to turn into bread.

This bleak road from Jerusalem to Jericho is where the story of the Good Samaritan is set. As we travelled on we saw in the distance a green oasis, which, as we approached, turned into Jericho. We passed just one sycamore tree: "Could this have been the one Zacchaeus climbed to see Jesus?" I wondered.

At an archaeological dig we saw remains, which could have been some of the original walls that Joshua and his army walked round for six days and then, on the seventh, demolished with a shout.

On we went to the Dead Sea and, as a typical tourist, David dutifully tried to swim in it. He found he could float in almost a sitting position without any effort. When, by accident, he got a few drops of the sea in his mouth, he said it was revolting. It has so many chemicals in it it tastes foul and it stung his face.

There was a beauty treatment available on the beach, many people smothered themselves with the black mud that was all around – it was supposed to be good for the skin – then after a while they showered it off. I didn't fancy a mud bath – particularly as it smelt foul. All I did was to paddle, that was enough for me.

Massada is a rocky mountain fortress now reached by cable car. Our guide issued a warning "Drink plenty of water it is very hot here, you don't want to get heatstroke!" There was a siege at Massada during the Roman occupation in which the Jews who had taken refuge there, rather than succumb to the Romans, or starve to death, or die of thirst, killed themselves.

We had a very good Israeli guide on our trip, called Joseph. He was a Jew, but not particularly religious, and an officer in the army. As we travelled around, he kept proclaiming, "How lucky you are, you are seeing flowers in the desert".

This is quite an unusual sight, which happens only every few years. The flowers did not seem so wonderful to us, as they were mainly small wild ones, some of which we might consider to be weeds, but their flowering in Israel depends on the amount of rain they had in the winter.

One morning we came out of our hotel to find a camel and its owner by the front steps. The camel driver asked, "Would you like to sit on the camel and take photographs." One of our Northern Irish colleagues nicknamed the camel Shergar, as it was soon after the famous racehorse Shergar's disappearance. Someone wisely asked, "How much is it to get on the camel?"

The camel owner, smiling broadly, said, "Nothing, but you'd better ask how much it is to get off!"

The next part of our trip took us to Tiberias, situated on the Lake of Tiberias, better known as the Sea of Galilee. On the way we visited Nazareth, a fairly ordinary looking sprawling town where Jesus grew up. Then to Capernaum where He ministered a lot. In Capernaum we saw the ruins of the Synagogue, which was adorned with the most beautiful purple Bougainvillea.

Galilee is beautiful, rolling green countryside surrounding a blue sea. I was immediately translated back in my imagination to the New Testament stories of Jesus preaching, teaching and healing.

Travelling to the Church at the top of Mount Tabor, the traditional Mount of Transfiguration, was an adventure in itself. We were packed into a fleet of Mercedes taxis and transported up the steep zigzag road. There were precipitous drops at the side of the road. As I was seated at the outside by a door I had to keep my eyes firmly fixed on the road ahead to keep my terror at bay. At the summit was a beautiful church with panoramic views of the valley of Jezreel below.

We had a boat trip on the Sea of Galilee to Ein Gev. The sea was calm all the time we were there, so it was hard to imagine that there could ever have been a storm like the one Jesus stilled. We were assured, however, that due to the situation of the lake within the surrounding hills, sudden squalls are a frequent occurrence. Back at our hotel that evening we had a meal of St Peter's fish caught in the Sea of Gallilee. They tasted a bit like plaice but were very bony.

The River Jordan is quite shallow in parts, but certain deeper areas are set aside for baptisms and we saw groups of pilgrims taking advantage of that facility. It was not difficult to be transported back in time and imagine John the Baptist calling to people to "Repent!" and it took one more step of imagination to think of Jesus there too being baptized

The Golan Heights are bleak and we were told of modern day victories, which could only be explained as miraculous. We were blocked from travelling through Samaria because of the troubles.

The Church of the Beatitudes overlooking the Sea of Galilee is a simple modern church but very beautiful. It is a place of calm and tranquillity. We paddled in the Sea of Galilee close by – and I have a photograph to prove it!

Banias is the modern day name for Caesarea Philippi and the archaeologists are digging a lot in that area. It was on the way there that Peter made his momentous declaration to Jesus "*You are the Christ, the son of the Living God.*" Matthew 16 verse 16.

On our way to Tel Aviv, where we would spend our last night on Israeli soil, we passed through Acre (mentioned in the Bible as Akko), which is a port that the Crusaders made the capital of their kingdom.

Soon however, we came back into the 20th century as we came through Haifa, Israel's main port and a sprawling city.

Our way led on through the other Caesarea (not Philippi) mentioned several times in the Acts of the Apostles. Much of what has been excavated there, including a massive amphitheatre, was of Roman origin so it was there in the time of Jesus.

To the south of Tel-Aviv is the small ancient port of Jaffa (Joppa in the Bible). Joppa is mentioned in both the old and new Testaments. Joppa is the port from which Jonah got the ship to run away from God. It was in Joppa that 'Simon the Tanner', who is mentioned in Acts, lived.

We lunched at several Kibbutzim as we travelled around Israel. In some we were well served and felt welcome, in others we were barely tolerated. The work that some of these Kibbutzim do to irrigate and fertilize the desert areas is amazing. It reminded me of texts in the Old Testament where God promises that the deserts will blossom.

When we travel David and I tend to notice different things – he will notice the big things, mountains and such like, I will notice insects, flowers and birds. In Israel I saw the smallest ants I've ever seen in our bathroom at Tel Aviv – about a quarter of the size of our ants, and also the biggest, about four times as big as ours, on the beach at Tel Aviv.

11 days is not long to form an impression of a land such as Israel but the overall impression was of holiness – despite all the problems and the commercialisation.

There were things, sometimes quite small, that I saw or experienced, that will always enhance my understanding of the Bible. We saw the 'lilies of the field' that Jesus talked about. We now understand the importance of foot washing as we have seen the dusty terrain and felt the heat. We saw sheep, shaggy and blotched with brown or black, and the goats, also shaggy and blotched with brown or black. They graze together and look so much alike that it is difficult to sort out one from another. In Matthew chapter 25 v 32 Jesus talks about the final judgement how all people will be separated into two groups, *'just as a shepherd separates the sheep from the goats.'* I had always thought this would be an easy exercise as British sheep and goats generally look so different from each other. Not so with Israeli sheep and goats.

Then there was the cell in Caiaphas' house where Jesus probably spent the night before the crucifixion, a hole in the ground with no window or light where he would have been thrown for the night. Was this just one more misery and indignity that He had endured?

We spent time in Jerusalem the Golden and on the Mount of Olives and can perhaps understand a little better why Jesus wept over Jerusalem with all its racial and religious tensions. We saw the beauty of Galilee and imbibed the whole atmosphere of the Holy Land.

Our travelling companions from Ulster were very nice people and welcomed us amongst them. During our time together we learned more about the Northern Irish problems and met with some of the bigotry. Some of them complained bitterly at having to enter yet another Catholic church and others flatly refused to go inside. Because of their age, most of the churches there are either Catholic or Orthodox. On one occasion two very earnest young men from our party cornered us, on a sofa in our hotel lounge. They spent time trying to convince us of the rightness of their Loyalist cause. We found it quite threatening.

All the time we were in Israel we were aware of the presence of God and appropriate Bible passages were read at each stopping place. It was a tiring trip but a wonderful experience. As we travelled home He was still with us.

We arrived late at Heathrow and then had to get to Euston for a train home. As we got there the last train for Crewe that night was about to leave. Crewe is about 20 miles from Knutsford but there was no train going any nearer that night. We had to run down the platform toting our luggage to get it. We hoped we would be able to get a taxi for those last 20 miles.

The problem was that we had not allowed for getting a taxi for 20 miles in our budget. I was so tired that once we were on the train I prayed and put the matter into God's hands. Then I relaxed and determined not to worry about it but enjoy this last leg of our journey home.

It was good to get home and see Sally and Pop again. When we looked through our post there was a cheque from the tour company for exactly the amount of our taxi fare. They said we had not been able to go on a trip that was included in the original itinerary. The cheque was a refund. We never did work out what we had missed out on. We praise God for our trip to Israel and God's provision for us.

Angelic Guidance.

'For he will command his angels concerning you to guard you in all your ways.' Psalm 91 verse 11

When Sally was taking A Levels we started looking around for a college where she could take a degree. She thought she might become a teacher but wanted to keep her options open. Her mock results were not outstanding so she did not think she would have enough points for a University place. Her actual results were much better.

One college she chose to look at was near Birmingham. I have driven a car for many years, but have been spoilt by a husband who usually drives to new places or busy cities. I tend to panic if I do not know exactly where I am going or where I will park. Cities are usually full of one-way systems and my poor sense of direction leaves me completely in this kind of situation. We started our round of colleges by driving to Birmingham.

I prayed specifically, that God would guide us that day. The college was on the outskirts of Birmingham and Sally would be there for several hours. We found the college and Sally was delivered safely for her interview. I drove on into Birmingham where I planned to do some window-shopping and get lunch. I found myself near the Bull Ring, but where could I park? It was then that God sent my first 'angel'. He was an ordinary man, but I felt he was my messenger from God. I could see a car park but couldn't see the entrance. My 'angel' was standing on an island in the middle of the road and directed me. He was there again at the entrance to the car park itself so there was no way I could miss it.

Once there I went off window shopping and got myself some lunch. It was time to retrace my steps to the college but first I needed to find the car. I must have looked a bit uncertain of myself because the second 'angel' appeared and asked, "Can I help you? Are you lost?" and directed me safely back to the car park.

I found my way back to the college picked Sally up and returned to Knutsford without further incident, Praise the Lord!

After investigating several colleges Sally had an offer from St Martin's College in Lancaster and studied R.E. and Social Ethics there and gained a good Degree.

CHAPTER SEVEN

Into the Valley

Change of Life

*'"Meaningless! Meaningless!" says the Teacher. "Utterly
meaningless! Everything is meaningless."'* Ecclesiastes 1 verse 2

It was after Sally went away to college in 1984 that my life began to change so drastically.I felt as though my purpose for living had gone. We still had Pop and the dog but the children that I had spent a good part of my life caring for and bringing up were both gone, Martin dead and Sally away, at least most of the time.

I began to ask myself, "What shall I do with the rest of my life? What is my purpose for living?" I trace the beginnings of my depression to this time. It was at this time that being a woman, my body decided to begin changing too.

We did quite quickly get used to Sally being away most of the time, and although we missed her, it had compensations. Her father could actually get into the shower most mornings for one thing, and the washing machine breathed a sigh of relief- until half term when it had to get into its stride again. Her room too remained tidy. When she was at home the room varied between super tidy and a tip.

In the summer of 1985 the depression deepened. Twenty-five years of bringing up children, now what? Careers were not thought important for girls when I was young, so I had no career to go back to. In any case I knew my parents could not keep me on at school longer than 16 they needed a contribution to the household purse. What should I do with my time now?

I did experience a call, in February 1984, to write a book. It happened like this, one morning when I was between waking and sleeping, God said, "Doreen, I want you to write a book about the gifts of the Holy Spirit."

(I think God chose that time, as it was only then that I was quiet enough to listen.) My first reaction was to argue that many people had already done that (and much more learned and well known people than me), but, on the other hand, it would be something that I would love to do.

A few days later when I was praying with a friend, I asked her to pray with me that God would confirm that what I thought he had asked me to do, really was his will. I didn't tell her what it was then. I was currently reading a chapter a day from Corrie ten Boom's book *Clippings from my Notebook*. The next morning I picked it up and started reading, the first sentence was '*My nephew, Peter van Woerden, and I wrote a book . . .*'

I now had enough confirmation to begin to think out and plan the book. I began to enjoy it – though it was hard work and took discipline. I could always see something that needed doing in the house and put off going into the study for another ten minutes.

This was an important step for me and I looked for a third confirmation for this project. This came on the 1st Saturday in May when I attended the Cheshire chapter of the F.G.B.M.F.I. (Full Gospel Business Men's Fellowship International) breakfast.

One speaker was a man from the St Helens chapter of F.G.B.M.F.I. He told how the chapter had started and his involvement in it. He said "I was living in Mid Cheshire when one morning when I was half awake and half asleep God spoke to me and told me to move to Bold. I didn't even know where Bold was then but soon discovered it was near St Helens."

So, I thought to myself, God does speak to people when they are half awake and half asleep, – my third confirmation.

After the breakfast I spoke to the man and thanked him for sharing and said "God spoke to me when I was half awake and half asleep."

"What did he ask you to do?" he asked.

"Write a book about the Holy Spirit".

"Let's pray for that".

He proceeded to pray for God's inspiration, God's timing, the publication, the advertising, in fact he covered every area connected with the writing and publication of a book.

With hours of hard work this had been done and it had been duly sent off to publishers – but rejected. I asked for a reason why it was not fit for publication and was told they enjoyed my examples but not the categorical way the whole book had been written.

I did start to write an autobiography as most of the instances mentioned had come from my own experience. "But who would want to read about me, I'm not someone rich or famous?" I was finding writing difficult anyway because it meant spending a lot of time on my own and I was getting more and more depressed. I felt I needed to be with people.

I was not working then, as the job in the bookshop had gone when the shop was sold after a marriage break up. In October 1985 David asked if I would like to work 2 days a week with him. They needed an extra typist – that at least was one skill I had to offer. It did me good to get out and learn new skills; whilst there I learnt to use the Dictaphone, switchboard and word processor. It did wonders for my confidence; I had some use in the outside world.

The depression did not, however, leave me but deepened until one day when Pop did something I thought stupid and I screamed at him. I totally over-reacted and knew that I would have to do something about how I was feeling.

When I saw the doctor he put me on anti-depressants. I wasn't very happy about taking pills. Taking pills for a sore throat or heart trouble or something physical seemed okay, but taking them for depression seemed like a defeat, particularly for a Christian who believes in healing. I felt guilty taking pills. A friend who works in the drug industry was cross with my attitude and said "What's wrong with taking pills to correct the balance of chemicals in the brain if the imbalance is making you unwell". Put like that it did seem to make sense. So I took them and also had prayer whenever the opportunity arose.

Facing Loss Again

'My soul is weary with sorrow strengthen me according to your word.' Psalm 119 verse 28.

Over the years, when thinking about the possibility that one day my parents would die, I have always thought that it would not be too difficult a bereavement. Hopefully, they would be old and everyone must die sometime, but losing a parent is a bereavement, and bereavement means pain in one form or another.

My father had been unwell for two years, though not really ill all that time. We had been told that he had Parkinson's disease and we knew his kidneys were not functioning too well. Just before we were due to go on holiday in August 1986 my sister rang to say Dad was going into hospital. His physical problems had been getting worse and his mind had been going and he was doing strange things. Dad, normally a shy, modest man took to undressing at inappropriate times and inappropriate places.

We were assured that it wasn't a life-threatening situation, so we went off on holiday, ringing home frequently. The rest did us good but our anxiety about Dad took the edge off our full enjoyment. As soon as we got home I planned to go and visit him but developed a streaming cold so I had to postpone it. By the time I was fit enough to go he had already died. On top of all that was wrong with him Dad, like Martin, had developed pneumonia and that was just one thing too much.

Dad was a Christian – despite his doubts during and after the war. Since retirement he had come back to the church and while he was in hospital he could often be heard singing hymns remembered from childhood. He did not have a wonderful singing voice so it probably drove the other patients and staff mad!

I had lived at a long distance from Dad for most of my married life, so the loss of Dad was not as drastic as the loss of Martin. It did not impinge on our daily life. It took a while to actually sink in that there was another 'hole' in the family. The funeral was a quiet affair where we sang Dad's favourite hymn '*The day Thou gavest Lord is ended*' which was also very appropriate.

Our greatest concern now was for Mum. How would she manage on her own? She was desperately lonely and in a state of shock. Her forgetfulness began to increase.

What do I miss most about my Dad? I think probably his sense of humour. He could be a terrible tease and at times came out with awful puns. He never showed his affection for us girls in a particularly physical way with hugs, but we knew he cared. He was a very intelligent, rather timid and fearful man, lacking in confidence. My husband reckons I'm like him in that way, which I will concede is probably right.

Dad loved words and would enjoy his daily crossword. Whenever we were together we played Scrabble and though others played with us, it would often develop into a competition between Dad and me. He never quite forgave me for using the word 'zonulets' to gain some fantastic score and win the game! 'Zonulets' became a byword for cheating in the family, although it had been used perfectly legitimately originally.

Soon after Dad's death we began to talk about two more possible changes in our lives. I saw some new houses being built in another part of the town. They were a lot smaller than where we were living and I fancied one of them. The other thing was our concern for Pop's future, he was now eighty-two and although he suffered with emphysema, he was fairly fit and able to look after himself. We had to face the possibility that this would not always be so and wondered how both he, and I, would cope if he could no longer bath himself, or needed other personal care and attention.

We discussed it with him and made enquiries about old peoples homes. We soon discovered that to get into these homes residents had to be able to fend for themselves and be in reasonable health, otherwise it had to be a nursing home. Pop fulfilled their requirements. I had mixed feelings about these enquiries, feeling almost like a traitor, as though we were abandoning Pop at a time in his life when he might need us most.

In the meantime we looked into the possibility of moving – with just three of us, and a dog most of the time, a smaller house did seem to be an option. David was not convinced, but I liked the idea. The houses we were looking at had four bedrooms and a study downstairs. They had the same number of rooms that we already had, just everything except the kitchen was smaller. The gardens were smaller; there was less paint-work, less maintenance in every way.

We decided to 'test the waters' by putting our house on the market and a deposit on the plot for the new house. David was understandably cautious, as our last move had cost us fifteen months of bridging loan and heartache. This time we had three offers for the asking price for our house during the first week it was advertised, so we decided to go ahead.

Our enquiries on Pop's behalf were going forward too and he was accepted into a Local Preachers Mutual Aid home down in Hertfordshire – these homes were run specifically for elderly Local Preachers in the

Methodist Church or their relatives. There, he would be nearer to the other part of his family than he had been for the last 17 years. He moved in April and was settled before our move.

At the same time we were tussling with another problem. Our dog, by now so much a part of the family and getting rather elderly, had damaged a tendon in one back leg. He did this while sprinting away from an old enemy, a border collie called Pip, who had bitten him rather badly on the ear when he was a pup. After treatment and a couple of weeks to recover he did exactly the same with the other leg by sprinting away from Pip again. He was almost grounded on his rear end.

We took him back to the vet and half expected him to say there was nothing he could do, but he gave us some more pills and suggested that we supported his rear with a sheeting sling. We must have presented a very strange picture walking along the road almost carrying Skipper's rear end. Once the pills were finished we could see that he was still very much in pain and took him back to the vet for what we thought would probably be the last time. It proved to be so, and we will never forget the look of reproach on Skipper's face as we left the vet to give him the final injection.

God's timing did not seem too good to me. Sally went back to college on the Friday, we took Pop to Rickmansworth to live on the Saturday, then we had to have Skipper put to sleep on the Tuesday. I felt so empty; it was good that we had the move to think about. But coping with so many changes when you are depressed is not a good idea – I didn't know whether I was on my head or my heels.

The depression deepened and we were both very tired. There was so much to organize. A friend, a real Job's comforter, cheered me up by saying, "Moving house is rather like having a baby, after a while you forget how terrible it was so you move again, only to discover how awful it really is!"

The moving date was set for 28th May but would the house actually be ready? It certainly didn't look like it, and even if the house itself were ready, would the removal van be able to get down the potholed muddy lane, which was currently our road?

The day before the move we arranged for the burglar alarm fitter to come and then, later in the day, the carpet fitters. Unfortunately, after the burglar alarm fitter had finished and gone, the carpet fitters managed to nail through one of the wires. This set off the alarm so we had to get the alarm fitter back again very quickly. I thought of the Flanders and Swann song 'It all makes work for the working man to do'.

The day of the move BT rang to tell us that we would not be able to have the 'phone connected in the new house – there was no cabling in. They had known about our move for five weeks and only notified us that day. We had five weeks without a 'phone which made it very difficult keeping in touch with Sally, Mum and Pop.

Another frustration that day was that no one came from the Gas Board to disconnect our gas fire and yet three men called to fit it at the new house. In the end David escorted the third man to the other house to disconnect it and take it back to the new house and fit it there.

A new stage in our life had begun. Our new house was nice although David called it 'pokey'. It had it's share of teething problems one of which was that one light switch turned the hall, landing and bathroom lights on and off which made for interesting bath times!

We did not enjoy living on a building site, particularly during the first few weeks as the rain was incessant and turned the site into a quagmire. Hardy friends set out to visit us, and most of them managed to get through, even though they ruined shoes to do it. Some, less determined, turned back, no doubt thinking that no one could be foolhardy enough to live in such a place, they must surely have got the address wrong! The milkman wouldn't venture down our road but delivered our milk to a house on the main road. The dustmen didn't find us for weeks either which meant regular visits to the tip. The Doctor tried to visit us but found his way blocked by a bulldozer. He gave up and came later – fortunately, it was not an emergency.

About a fortnight after we moved in David had to go away for two nights. We were still the only residents on this part of the estate and the 'phone was still not connected. In my depression I panicked and wondered how I would cope. I thank God for good Christian friends who looked after me and allowed me to use their phone.

But God was still looking after me. The day David left the car went wrong – the brakes were binding, so I had to take it to be repaired. I drove cautiously to the garage and while I was booking it in I had to give my name and address. When I said "23", a voice beside me said "Hollingford Place". It was Jon Hutchings who was soon to be our next-door neighbour. He'd brought his car in for repair too but had a hired car waiting for him so I got a lift back home.

The worst was not over. David had to go away again, this time for eight days at the end of June. I dreaded the thought of him going. This may seem strange to you, a grown woman dreading being on her own, but I had never been on my own before in my life. As a child there was always someone there. Once we'd married we had Pop with us, and then the children, so I found being on my own very frightening. At least the 'phone was connected just before he left but even then I felt I could not stay on my own overnight. Friends, Sheila and Geoffrey, offered me a bed each night that I gladly accepted and went home during the day. It came at a bad time too as the doctor had reduced my antidepressants from four a day down to two and I was not coping very well.

With prayer and care I managed those eight days and even found there could be advantages in being on my own. I could eat what I liked and when I liked, I could have my choice of TV programmes. There are always advantages and disadvantages in all situations.

Throughout the depression I found that God, often through his people, was still very active in my life. Perhaps that is one big lesson I am meant to learn from depression, that God is not a feeling and not dependent upon our feelings, he is at work no matter how we feel.

Some incidents, which happened in connection with our holiday that year, will show you what I mean. Early in 1987 before we had decided to move we had booked to go on holiday to Paignton in Devon for a week at the end of July.

The first inkling we had of God's involvement in our holiday plans was about ten days before we were due to go. I was visiting an elderly friend, Verlie, whose husband had recently died. We talked a lot and during the conversation she said, "My cousin has asked me to go and visit her in Totnes. I don't think I can go because I don't want to drive all that way. I don't know how well we will get on together either, I haven't seen her for years."

In my ignorance I asked, "Where is Totnes?"

"It's in Torbay" she replied.

I didn't know a lot about Paignton but I did know it was in Torbay and I laughed, recognizing this as something of God's planning. We took her with us and we all enjoyed our stay in Devon.

This was not the only coincidence (I prefer to call it a God incident) to occur in connection with this holiday. On the way down we decided to stop off in Exeter to see an elderly uncle of David's in an old people's home there. We found him very frail and bedridden but although he was very tired and wondering why he had lived so long, he was glad to see us. He told his daughter we'd been but couldn't remember our names.

We were so glad we decided to visit on the way down because after we got home we had a phone call to say that he'd died on the Friday of our holiday week. If we'd left it till the return journey we would have been too late. God's timing is perfect and He is active no matter how we are feeling. Praise His name!

God at Work

'Do not hide your face from me when I am in distress. Turn
your ear to me; when I call answer me quickly.'
Psalm 102 verse 2

Pat had been wondering for some time about being baptized by total immersion. She felt it was something God wanted her to do.

She asked me "Will you think and pray about where and when I could be baptized? I don't feel right about going to another church but I know it isn't possible in ours."

After about a year no decision had been made and no date set. Then another mutual friend Joyce, declared, "God has told me to be baptized!"

Whereas Pat did not mind waiting, on the other hand Joyce wanted it NOW! So we prayed and thought how we could arrange it. At least it was August and we could have it outside. There is a mere in Tatton Park, which is in Knutsford, and in certain parts bathing is allowed, so a group of us decided to take the two women into the park and baptize them there.

The afternoon we chose turned out warm and sunny and we found an ideal spot. It was so beautiful we could almost imagine we were beside the Sea of Galilee. We read a passage from the New Testament about baptism then prayed and baptized them. It was a time of blessing for all of us and I felt privileged to be involved.

~

Despite the fact that I was still depressed we decided to have Mum and Pop to stay. I'm glad we did because this turned out to be the last time we were to have either of them to stay. They were with us for a week. Mum was already suffering from the early symptoms of senile dementia and inclined to be forgetful. Pop was mentally alert but very breathless with emphysema. Mum had the physical fitness, Pop the mental alertness, so they looked after each other for the two days I worked.

I managed to handle their visit but could now do nothing outside my regular job and looking after our home. Anything like a prayer meeting or even a social gathering left me weak, shaky or weepy. If I was out in an evening I would be unable to sleep for hours afterwards because the adrenalin would still be flowing and my mind too active. The only thing to do, for the moment, was to opt out and rest. It was not an easy decision to make or stick to, I have always made myself do things, it seemed to me that it was admitting weakness not to.

I thought the depression probably had not only mental and physical causes, but possibly spiritual causes as well. With the spiritual in mind, the Thursday after Mum and Pop had gone home, I felt I would like to talk to our Minister. I hesitated to ring him because I knew how busy he was. It is very difficult to make even simple decisions when you are suffering with depression. If you can, you shelve them or give them to someone else to make. In this case I prayed and gave the problem to the Lord. "Well, if you want me to see Graham", I prayed, "you'll have to send him here."

Once again God showed me his great sense of humour and care. Having forgotten all about that prayer I was surprised by a ring at the front door at about 4.30 p.m. it was Graham, our Minister. He had not come to see me but to give me a message for David, but he stayed and talked and prayed with me and anointed me with oil for healing. Graham was very helpful, as he understood depression as he had suffered with it himself.

The following week I had another example of God's timing and his sense of humour. It was as I was praying on Thursday as I got on with the housework that I said, "Lord we haven't had many callers lately, we had a lot when we first moved in but they don't come anymore. Well, Lord, it's your house not ours when are you going to use it?"

You really have to be careful what you say to God, because he will take you up on anything you say, as I was soon to find out in this instance! Later in the day I received a 'phone call. The caller was Elizabeth who said, "A group of students from Cliff College are coming next weekend and a family has had to withdraw from entertaining one of them. I have been praying and David and your names kept coming to me, could you possibly help me out?"

I laughed and told her about my prayer and said, "In the circumstances we'll be delighted".

The week the students came was a busy one with two consecutive evenings out, and they arrived on Friday evening.

Our visitor was a young Australian woman. She had been trained as a vet, but after she became a Christian felt she was called to a musical ministry. She certainly had a wonderful musical ministry, which we experienced while she was with us. As we talked together over meals that weekend, there were several God incidents we shared, not least that she was just recovering from a bout of severe depression. We knew God had put us together for a purpose – if only to share our experience.

The Cliff College students started a coffee bar project at our church where David acted as occasional 'bouncer' – a very unlikely role for him, and I stayed in the background and prayed.

Joy and Sadness

'Do not be yoked together with unbelievers. For what do righteousness and wickedness have in common? Or what fellowship can light have with darkness?'
2. Corinthians 6 verse 14

By October of 1987 Sally had gained her degree in Religious Education and Social Ethics and went back to study for her Post Graduate Certificate in Education so that she could become a teacher.

The most important thing that happened in that first term was that she met the man who was shortly to become her husband. He had a maths degree and, after taking a year out to try and get into the Yorkshire Fire Brigade, he decided to take a PGCE at St Martins too. He attended the same church as Sally – then called the Lancaster Christian Fellowship, now the Kings Community Church.

We soon began to hear about this young man and in November Sally said, "I really want you to meet Simon. Can you come up on Sunday after Church and we could meet you for lunch?"

We did not need a second bidding and when we met we got on very well with Simon and we could see they were very happy together. Simon must have made an impression on David as when we were driving home he said of Simon, "I didn't think they made them like that anymore."

Things were not going so well in Rickmansworth where Pop became ill, his breathing deteriorated rather badly and in mid-December he was taken into hospital to establish him on oxygen. It was close to Christmas when he was in the ambulance on the way back to the home that he had a heart attack and was dead on arrival back at the hospital. He was 83, which is a good age, but we missed him.

We had already arranged to spend Christmas with David's brother, Cliff and his wife Joan in Chingford, so we went. Sally went with us to Chingford but missed Simon so much that the telephone got red hot.

The earliest date possible for Pop's funeral was 5 January. It was a quiet family funeral held at his home church in Chingford. He and his wife had been founder members, when they moved there soon after they married. A previous minister from Knutsford, Rev Derek Davidson, who conducted Martin's funeral and knew Pop well, came up from his current post in Leatherhead to help with the service.

This was a strange bereavement for me as, in all honesty, I had felt bereft when Pop had first gone to the home in April. He had lived with us from the day we married so he was always there. When he moved out I realized how much I had come to rely on him. He always had plenty of time and was a good listener. David was always busy and wasn't a good listener. He's getting better with practice!

Although it is inhibiting to have a parent around, it does mean that you always have someone to turn to for advice, even if you never take it! Even so, while he was in the home in Rickmansworth, I could phone him if I wanted to, but now he was gone.

While David and I were adjusting to Pop's death, Sally and Simon's romance flourished. Sally had had boyfriends before, but we sensed that this was different. Simon is a Christian and Sally had always declared she would only marry a Christian. She rang just before Easter to say, "I want to bring Simon home for Easter, he has something to ask you". We didn't have to be geniuses to guess what!

We had a full house that Easter as Joan and Cliff were coming too. Simon did the courteous thing and asked David if he could marry Sally. They became engaged that Easter.

We had agreed to the engagement the next question was "When do you want to get married?"

"August," said Sally.

"August 1989?"

"No, this August."

They wanted to marry in just four months time – we thought it was much too soon. Neither of them had jobs, and Simon had just dropped out of his teaching course. He failed his teaching practice and, although he could have taken it again he felt he just would not make a teacher. Sally's course didn't finish until July. They had not known each other very long either. David and I knew each other four and a half years before we married.

"Mum", Sally said, "What's the point of setting up home on our own, we've each got to find somewhere to live while we look for jobs? If we get married we can set up home together and look for jobs together."

As they talked to us it did make sense. We were thankful that they did intend to get married before they set up home together.

We talked a lot that Easter. As far as we were concerned, financially, it could have been a better year for a wedding. We had already planned and paid for a rather expensive trip to Greece in the Steps of St Paul in June. It was too late to cancel it without losing our money.

They wanted the wedding in Lancaster where many of their friends were and where they hoped to make their home. In the end we agreed providing we could find a good place for the reception. This seemed to be the most difficult of the facilities to book. We tried the hotels in and around Lancaster; they were all booked but one recommended a hotel in Morecambe that had just finished refurbishing. They were just starting to take bookings again. We tried there and the only Saturday they had free in August was the 13th so we booked it there and then.

The panic was on, but having such a short time to organize things does concentrate the mind wonderfully. Soon the bridesmaids were booked, Hannah, Simon's niece from Northumberland, Marion, Sally's friend from Cheshire and Nicola, Sally's cousin from Essex. We met Simon's parents and together organized the guest list.

Sally is very particular about her clothes, when she was in her teens I would have to be very patient as we trailed from shop to shop. A quick scan from the doorway and she knew she would not find anything she liked in that shop. I knew she would be very particular (and rightly so) about her wedding dress.

As soon as we had a spare day we set off to explore the shops and bridal agencies in the area. The nearest to Knutsford was a bridal agency operating from a farmhouse. Sally tried on two or three dresses there. The first was a beautiful pure silk ivory Victorian style dress, which looked beautiful on her tall slim figure (she is 5 feet 11 inches tall). Although she really liked it and it suited her figure and colouring, she felt she could not buy the first dress she tried on, so we spent the rest of the day travelling to all the bridal shops we knew. Late in the day we returned to the agency and bought the dress. We would not have been able to afford it if it had been brand new.

The bridesmaids' dresses were peach and chosen by taking just our local bridesmaid, Marion, to a shop, together with the measurements of the other two. When we gathered again in Manchester for a fitting the only dress, which did not fit was Marion's! It was finally ready just days before the wedding.

It was just 5 weeks before the wedding that Simon found a temporary job and a house to rent.

We, and many of our guests, stayed at the reception hotel the night before the wedding and Sally went from there to the church. We gathered at St Martin's College chapel for the wedding, which was conducted by the Pastor from their Fellowship.

The wedding day was lovely in everything but weather. The service was a lively, happy affair and the bride and groom made a handsome couple (but then I'm biased aren't I?) and the bridesmaids did them credit. Like her mother before her she had chosen fresh flowers for hers and the bridesmaids head-dresses and bouquets. As they came out of the chapel for the photographs it began to rain and steadily got worse until it was a downpour. The photographer was ready for this, supplying us with large white umbrellas. Unfortunately, the group photographs are rather thin as everyone disappeared to the reception as the rain worsened.

Unbeknown to most of the guests Sally and Simon spent the first night of their honeymoon in the reception hotel leaving early next morning in my car for the island of Jura. Arriving later than expected at the ferry they saw it disappearing and with very little spare money they had to find accommodation for the night. They arrived on Jura next day where there were more sheep and deer than people, but then who needs other people when you are on honeymoon?

CHAPTER EIGHT

To Greece in the Steps of St Paul

Our Second Pilgrimage

*'Paul then stood up in the meeting of the areopagus and said;
"Men of Athens! I see that in every way you are very religious.
For as I walked around and looked carefully at your objects of
worship, I even found an altar with this inscription: TO AN
UNKNOWN GOD. Now what you worship as something
unknown I am going to proclaim to you.' Acts 17 verse 22*

In the midst of our arrangements for the wedding the time came for our
trip to Greece. It was a good holiday but very tiring. The depression was
still there and difficulties that should have been minor became problems
to me. We did, however, see some interesting places with a very nice
group of people.

We travelled to Thessalonica via London and Athens and after a late
evening meal walked along beside the sea. The promenade was very busy
and cars and motorbikes used it like a racetrack. The road surface seemed
dangerously smooth and none of the motorcyclists wore helmets.

Our guide on this trip was Eugeni. She was very nice and a positive
mine of information. Unfortunately, she imparted it all the time until in
the end you couldn't take any more in and switched off!

Next day we set off from our hotel to view the lion of Amphipolis.
This animal had been rather like a massive jigsaw puzzle. Pieces were
found by archaeologists and put together, then after the animal had been
completed, more pieces had been found indicating that maybe it should
have been even larger.

We went on to the museum, where we saw beautiful golden artefacts,
caskets, wreaths and other jewellery. One piece that particularly fascinated
me was a magnificent wreath made in the shape of oak leaves and acorns.

The Ancient Greeks were very skilled in both intricate and delicate work as well as large stonework.

Kavala, a seaside town famous for wooden shipbuilding, was our next stop. There was an ancient aqueduct there; a wonderful feat of engineering but it was covered with weeds.

On we travelled to Philippi and the prison. There is a story in Acts 16 of Paul and Silas being gaoled there. During the night they were praying and singing hymns when there was an earthquake and they were set free, but they did not run away. The gaoler recognized that he had witnessed a miracle and he and his household became Christians.

By the White tower in Thessalonica there is an impressive larger than life statue of Alexander the Great.

As we passed the University Eugeni explained that she was a teacher and the teachers were on strike. We came across another strike when we went to Corinth.

She pointed out to us the hospital and then opposite the Orthodox cemetery with its elaborate tombs. Next-door was the Protestant cemetery with its much simpler tombs, next door to that was the Armenian cemetery. If I was ill in Thessalonica I would not find it very encouraging having the hospital so close to all the cemeteries!

The City wall, built 2,200 years ago and decorated in the 10th and 11th Centuries, was impressive but again very weedy. From the Acropolis wall we looked down over the whole of Thessalonica right down to the sea. As we drove through Thessalonica we passed through several areas that had been damaged in the 1978 earthquake. I had forgotten about that earthquake and reflected on how soon we forget about such disasters unless we are directly involved.

On then to the church of St Demetrius (Thessalonica Cathedral) The founder of the church, Leonides is said to have been unable to walk for 50 years, then one night on the eve of St Demetrius day, he dreamt that he would be able to walk. When he woke up he found he could walk. The church was built as a thanksgiving.

The church was magnificent but, whereas the Roman Catholics have their statues and candles, the Greek Orthodox have candles and icons. I sat and watched how the local people used this church, both men and women (though mostly women) came through and crossed themselves, some lit candles, some kissed icons, some said rosaries. Our driver, Alexei, an erstwhile Jehovah's Witness converted to Greek Orthodoxy, had his rosary with him all the time, even when he got off the coach for lunch and coffee.

St Paul's visit to Thessalonica had been much longer than ours and after preaching several times in the Synagogue, it ended in near riot, with Paul and Silas fleeing for their lives. Some people did believe and a church was born.

As you travel it is interesting to notice where and how differently other people live. Most city dwelling Greeks (that is the majority of the 10 million) live in apartments. In the country many of them live in 2 storey chalet type houses, some with flat roofs, and not a gutter in sight. They make use of solar power. We noticed a lot of partly built houses and churches that we asked Eugeni about. She told us that in Greece when someone has some money they start to build a house until the money runs out, only when they have more money do they continue. To build a church in this way it must be completed in 7 years but not so with a house – some of them looked as though they had been abandoned for years in their half completed state.

Close to the Yugoslav border is Pella where there are open flat ruins with mosaic floors and such like. It was very hot there with no shade at all. As I stood looking at the floor I noticed the remains of a snake being consumed by a trail of large ants, I shuddered, thankful that the snake was dead. This was the area of Greece where we saw paddy fields; I had not seen rice growing before.

Our meal at Edessa was fairly typical, and consisted of courgette stuffed with rice and meat with a sauce, this was followed by Moussaka with a salad of onion, cucumber, tomato, pepper, olive and dressing, this was followed by a sweet cake rather like syrup sponge pudding. Some of us had cups of tea forgetting to ask for no sugar – tea is automatically served sweetened in Greece.

There were some beautiful raging waterfalls and we were able to get behind one of them: amazing.

Our next stop was at Veria – Berea of the Bible. After they were chased out of Thessalonica this was the next place that Paul and Silas visited. Some of the Beroeans accepted the message and all went well until the

Thessalonian Jews realized what was happening and went there to cause trouble. This time Paul was sent on to Athens, while Silas and Timothy stayed on in Berea. There is a shrine to St Paul at the synagogue in Veria with a colourful mosaic of him. From there we could see for miles across the plain.

When we arrived in Kalambaka, in the area of Greece called Meteora, it was already dark, imagine our surprise when we woke next morning and looked out of the bedroom window to see massive mountainous stones of a kind of aggregate rock. It looks rather like the concrete we make, but it is natures own concrete. These rocks rise up from the plain in mounds as though dumped there by some careless giant. They are full of caves.

There are many monasteries set high on these mounds. They were built centuries ago without today's machinery. Most of the materials to build them were winched up in baskets with pulleys and ropes.

We climbed up to St Nicholas Anapavnas Monastery. As we ascended the final steps I looked down and saw a tortoise. On pointing this out to another member of the party I was informed that Greece was their natural habitat. I had never really thought where tortoises came from before; we'd got ours from the pet shop.

There were donkeys at the foot of the cliffs to carry weary travellers up to the monasteries. They didn't look big enough to carry a child, let alone a large adult, but we were assured that they could. It reminded me of my father who, when he was on leave in Egypt, during the war, went to the Valley of the Kings, travelling by donkey part of the way. We have a photograph of Dad, a large six-footer, on a tiny donkey with his feet almost touching the ground.

There were people selling cherries on the pathway and we bought some and shared them round, they were delicious and helped to quench our thirst.

We spent a long time looking at the pictures in the monastery chapel – they were everywhere and Eugeni described them in great detail.

Back at the hotel for lunch, David's face was a picture as we had courgettes yet again. He will eat them on sufferance at home, but in Greece, it was eat courgettes or starve!

After another long drive we arrived in Delphi. In its heyday the

Delphic Oracle was consulted over many problems. It always gave alternatives so that it was never wrong.

Delphi is a magnificent sight set on a hillside against a backdrop of brilliant blue skies. Several of the tall, slender cypress trees are set amongst beautiful ruins of arches, pillars, walls and floors.

In the museum there are magnificent statues. The likenesses were so individual and clear that you felt you would know them if you met them in the street. One was of a young boy who was said to be 'gay' and there was a bronze statue of a charioteer with particularly striking eyes.

Our long journeys in the coach meant that when we stopped we needed the convenience of toilets. On one occasion I entered the cubicle and closed the door only to find there was no handle on the inside. Panic set in, as there was no one else around at the time. Shouts of "Help, let me out!" rang out across the café until one member of our party heard me, otherwise I might still be there!

Our arrival in Athens at about 6 p.m. caused us much amusement as the Orientours representative was rather put out as he said "I expected you at 5.15 p.m."

We fell about laughing because the earliest we had arrived at any of the other hotels had been 9.30 p.m. we had always been later than expected by hours, not merely minutes.

After dinner at the respectable hour of 7.30 p.m. we went for a walk. Our hotel was very close to the Acropolis and we decided to walk round it. We got slightly lost and ended up going through narrow alleys which seemed more like going through people's gardens than a public thoroughfare.

Coming out into wider streets we passed tavernas where people were eating outside. Many of them were eating fish of various kinds. We had heard that fish was a speciality in Greece but seldom had it in our hotels it was always the ubiquitous moussaka.

In our wanderings we came upon Mars Hill where St Paul preached about the 'unknown God'. Then we came to a busy street of shops. It seemed like the place to shop for souvenirs if, that is, we ever stopped still long enough to have the time.

St Paul's reception in Athens was quite different from ours. In all probability he walked from Berea so it would have taken him much longer to get there. St Paul tried to speak to them from the point of their own understanding so, having seen a shrine to the 'unknown god', he spoke about the Christian God being this unknown god. When he talked about resurrection he was jeered and ridiculed but some wanted to know more and became Christians.

Early next morning we set off to go to Corinth over the Corinthian Canal, a magnificent feat of engineering.

I loved Corinth. It had been destroyed several times by earthquake and we know that it suffered turbulence during St Paul's time, but I felt God's presence and peace there – rather like the feeling I had in Jerusalem. We stood on the Bema, a kind of raised platform from where St Paul had preached. We had a short time of reading and prayer there, the reading was from 1 Corinthians 13, about love.

I knew Corinth had been a city of sin but I knew too that there had been a very powerful Christian witness. The Christians had actually taken over the pagan temples. Corinth is fairly flat, with one or two of the slender cypress trees standing out against a background of hills and brilliant blue sky.

St Paul preached very successfully in Corinth and stayed for eighteen months. The Corinthians in their enthusiasm got things wrong but they were a lively Spirit filled congregation.

I would have loved to stay longer and nearly had my wish, for as we approached the bridge over the Corinthian canal on our way back for lunch, followed by a 'free afternoon', we were stopped by the police. The agricultural workers were on strike and were blockading the bridge for four hours. They'd been there for one hour and had no intention for moving for another three.

I thought of Romans 8 v 8 '*All things work together for good for those that love God*' and wondered what God was going to do with this.

We were given a choice: back to Corinth or off to Mycene, another ancient site. The majority chose the latter so we went there stopping on the way for lunch. We found out afterwards that several of the group had been wondering how they could fit a trip to Mycene into our itinerary – the strikers did it for them.

Mycene is a burial site where there are enormous beehive-shaped tombs. The question we asked was "How did they build them?" as some of the individual stones weighed tons each.

In the evening we went to Son et Lumiere at the Acropolis. We sat on a hill about three quarters of a mile away from the Acropolis. Just the view from there of Athens all lit up was breathtaking, and then came the music, the story and the lights as the Parthenon came to life.

The story was of ancient Greece in the time of Xerxes. It included the burning of Athens. This was depicted with red lights rising and falling over the Parthenon.

We explored the Acropolis and the museum next day and found it bigger and more impressive than I had thought before. Sadly, pollution is damaging it and some steps have become warn, slippery and dangerous.

Having somehow carelessly lost some of our party, we went on our official visit to Mars Hill. To give a signal to the rest of our group we stood under a pine tree and sang 'And can it be', then 'Amazing grace'. It caused both amused and quizzical looks from other tourists and passing Greeks. Our signal did, however, have the desired effect, bringing back the wanderers who included both the tour guide and our leader. Their greeting was "I once was lost but now I'm found".

Our next trip was to Cape Sounion on the coast here there is another acropolis, the temple to Poseidon. Poseidon was the god of the sea and it was set on a promontory surrounded on 3 sides by the sea. By this time I was becoming quite blasé about 2 to 3,000-year-old buildings and columns.

We shopped that evening for souvenirs and then went to see Greek dancing and singing. The costumes were very colourful and smart and in several dances they joined men and women alternately in a line. David said it was like the 'Palais Glide' some of the singing was like the Fry's Turkish Delight advert on TV rather more like wailing than singing to Western ears.

On Sunday we shared Communion together and talked about what had blessed us so far on our holiday. We were due to travel on to a coastal resort called Lagonissi for the last few optional, relaxing, days of our holiday. We said farewell to a few of our number and then travelled on to the coast.

It was a holiday complex set on a promontory with hotel, restaurant, holiday bungalows and swimming pool. We only swam in the sea once, as the beach was rocky and sharp.

Sitting on our balcony on Monday morning overlooking the sea, directly below me was a fig tree and to the left two poplar trees with a colony of noisy sparrows. In Britain they nest singly but not in Greece.

Each morning we had prayers in the little site chapel (Greek Orthodox), a beautiful little white building with a bell and handy rope. David couldn't resist it and being the first there pulled it a few times. Inside, the chapel was full of little fancy lamps and icons. There were always a few lizards on the walls to join in our time of worship. It had a lovely peaceful, worshipful atmosphere.

In Lagonissi we had time to become aware of the wildlife around us, birds, lizards and butterflies, flowers and shrubs like Oleanders and Hibiscus.

We saw a very strange phenomenon one day as we sat around the pool; it was a rainbow in a complete circle around the sun, which was covered with hazy cloud. It was very eerie and stayed for a long time. It may well have been pollution.

For our final trip we were up at 5.45. a. m and on to a coach to Trogadera where we were to board the Aegean Glory for a trip to the three Greek Islands, Poros, Aegina and Hydra. As we approached the port there was a haze over the whole area – not, as we thought, a heat haze but air pollution. In an effort to reduce pollution, cars can be taken only on alternate days into Athens – it depends on your registration number which days you are allowed in.

We visited the island of Poros, then Hydra – it is so called because there is no water on the island at all. The land rose steeply behind the harbour and as we ate an ice cream at a back street taverna, three of our group who had decided to explore further came down the street on donkeys. We bought one of the hand-woven rugs there for a souvenir.

Back on board we had a late lunch and travelled on to Aegina. As we arrived we were shepherded on to dilapidated 1950s coaches and whisked away to the centre of the island to the temple of Aphia and Athena. This is a well-preserved temple made of limestone. It is placed in an equilateral triangle of 40 kilometres with Sounion and the Acropolis in Athens. Then back to the harbour and home on the 'Aegean Glory'.

On our last morning in Greece we had prayers again in the lovely little chapel, joined as usual by our lizard friends. We took this opportunity to pray and give thanks for our holiday.

Our homeward flight didn't inspire confidence as eight of us were asked to move to the back of the plane for take off. Once we were airborne we were allowed back to our original seats. It was something to do with the balance of the plane.

As we flew home I reflected on our visit to the sites of St Paul's missionary journeys and thought how much easier our visit had been. We found Greece a fascinating place steeped in history. The Ancient Greeks had such skills and abilities.

We came back to earth when we landed in Manchester and thought once again about the forthcoming wedding and all that still needed to be done.

CHAPTER NINE

Deeper into the Valley

Up, then Down Again

'Out of the depths I cry to you, O Lord.' Psalm 130 verse 1

Depression is an unpredictable illness and towards the end of 1988 I had come far enough out of it to be off the tablets. I had gone back to preaching too. Unfortunately, it did not last and in the early months of 1989 I fell back into that black hole.

The job at Methodist Insurance was disappearing with the coming of word processors, so I gave in my notice. I decided to try and get a local job. There were new things being started at our church during the day, which I wanted to be involved in too. I thought I could combine these with a local job. There was also the possibility of working at one of our country chapels as a pastoral assistant. They wanted me and I wanted to do it but felt unable to take it up yet because of the depression.

I started working part time at a travel firm in Knutsford but left there after only a few weeks. My main reason for leaving was because David was going off on trips, and I did not want to be left at home alone. At the time too I felt that God wanted me free from definite work commitments. I find it difficult to understand all these various decisions now. With hindsight I can say that I was probably deeper in depression than I realized. Decision-making is nigh on impossible when you are that depressed.

In May we went to Jersey for a fortnight. The first week should have been a working week for David, surveying the island's Methodist churches, and preaching on Sunday. The second week was to be a holiday.

We arrived in Jersey and were taken to pick up the hired car, as David lifted my suitcase (it had to be my suitcase!) into the car he became transfixed with an agonizing pain in his back. I managed to get him into the car and drove him, very cautiously, to the hotel where a doctor was called.

David was anxious because several years before he had to have a disintegrated disc taken out of his back, in what was quite a risky and painful operation.

On this occasion the doctor advised us that the only treatments necessary were painkillers and rest. Work plans and preaching had to be abandoned.

We were fortunate to have a ground floor room, with a sun lounge attached. David spent most of the first week lying flat out in the sun as he recovered. His speedy recovery must owe much to the prayers that were said for him by the visitors he had, both ministers and lay folk, from the local churches. By the second week he had recovered enough for us both to enjoy our holiday.

We were home from Jersey about a week then we were off again this time to Ireland for the Irish Methodist Conference.

We arrived at the quayside in Holyhead in good time for our trip to Dun Laoghaire. On presentation of our tickets we were asked, "What are you carrying?"

David replied, "A conference stand."

"Have you got a licence?" asked the customs official.

"No, should I have?"

"Yes, but we can issue one here."

It was a good job the sailing was delayed because of fog, as this licence turned out to be endless, made up of many copies with no carbon paper, each sheet had to be written independently.

We met a young family who had chosen to live in Ireland for the quality of life, fewer people, less traffic, more space altogether and they were happy with their choice. We noticed this ourselves once we travelled outside Dublin.

To pass the time on the crossing I went to see a film called 'My Stepmother is an Alien' which was very funny. There was a beagle in it called Dave who had a bark just like Skipper's after he had been in kennels. We only put Skipper in kennels once and he must have barked all the time he was there as he had hardly any bark at all when we collected him; he was totally hoarse. That is how Dave sounded all through the film.

We arrived later than expected in Dublin and we still had to get to

Nenagh in County Tipperary that evening and as everyone knows 'It's a long way to Tipperary!'

Once away from Dublin the journey was good with very little traffic. The road was not bad just 'corrugated' in parts. We arrived in Nenagh late in the evening, hungry, thirsty and tired. We had a light supper served with a glass of milk and then retired to bed. Milk is a speciality in Ireland and is offered at most meals.

In our room the heat and a noisy freezer somewhere below us made sleep impossible. In desperation, at 1 a.m. we asked for a room change. Sleep came much later.

A good cooked Irish breakfast set us up for our trip to Gurteen Agricultural College. This is set in a beautiful, peaceful spot and after the business was accomplished we had a superb lunch of home produced beef and vegetables followed by fruit crumble.

We continued our journey to the north till we came to the beautiful coastline of Co. Donegal and finally to Londonderry for the conference. In Londonderry we completely lost our way and found ourselves facing a notice, which said 'You are now entering free Derry'; we were in the Creggan. We asked the way to the church and a charming girl directed us.

We stayed across the river in the Protestant area of the city up the Limavady Road past the barracks. The barracks were enclosed by corrugated iron and barbed wire. Guarding the married quarters a few yards down the road were two pillboxes with soldiers on duty all the time.

Londonderry was a sad city divided by a beautiful river, and hatred and bigotry. In parts of the city the kerbstones were painted red, white and blue, other areas sported orange, white and green flags, but the conference folk made us welcome. We were shown proudly round St Columba's Cathedral where the apprentice boys are buried. There were many relics of the siege in there.

When I am away from home I look around for wool shops, I love looking for unusual knitting patterns. I found one in Londonderry and as I thumbed through the patterns the proprietor talked to me about the troubles. For many Northern Irish people the troubles not only cause pain and distress but also embarrassment. They like to explain.

She talked about the demonstrations which sparked them off in 1969. The Catholics were feeling left out as they were in the minority so they arranged civil rights marches. The police tried to squash these but they got too big for the police to handle so the army was brought in, and thirteen Catholics were shot. The underlying bitterness and hatred, which was there between the communities, rose to the surface. Londonderry became a place of hatred and fear. The situation has reversed since then as the Catholics are now in the majority and hold the positions of authority. The Protestants are now the ones feeling intimidated.

The troublemakers in Londonderry are, as always, a minority, and the majority would like to live in peace and safety. The shopkeeper was at pains to tell me she had friends in both communities.

While we were in Londonderry we saw soldiers on foot and in their peculiar armoured vehicles. As we came back from lunch one day four soldiers came down the road, guns at the ready, peering into flats and houses to make sure no one was taking pot shots at them. We stood still waiting for them to pass.

Walking around the City Centre, we were appalled by the number of shops, which had been destroyed by bombs. How people lived with the violence and tension day by day, I don't know. It made me realize how much they need our prayers. I am thankful for the steps towards peace that have been made since that time.

It was a busy but interesting time in Ireland, but David was at home for just 5 days before he had to be off again, this time to Leicester on his own for the British Methodist Conference. How was I going to cope with eight days and seven nights on my own? Having spent so much time travelling with him, eight days seemed, in my depressed state, like an eternity. Fears and anxiety overwhelmed me again. Normal things that I had to do seemed like enormous mountains that I had to climb.

David knew how I felt but he had to go. I planned to spend the nights staying with friends. David rang as often as he could and arranged for me to go down to Leicester for the last two days of the conference. The thought of travelling there on my own sent me into a panic but the way I was feeling, anything would have been preferable to staying in the house on my own a moment longer than necessary. I certainly could not get in the car and drive there, I had completely lost my nerve for driving.

I found that there was a coach, which went from Tabley (a small village just outside Knutsford) to Leicester. A friend said she would drive me there and in the event stayed with me until the coach arrived. All the way there I was anxious that I would miss David in Leicester. I need not have worried, because he was almost the first person I saw when we arrived. I don't remember much about those days in Leicester and when I returned home the fears and anxieties were still there.

Things which probably most of us fear but are usually in the background took over my mind: fear of death, fear of David's death, fear of being left alone, fear of illness, fear of God (an unhealthy fear not just respect or awe), fear of a gas leak (I have no sense of smell so it was logical, but again it was out of proportion). I felt very inadequate and thoroughly frightened. I could not sleep at night but lay awake in fear.

Some friends came for the day on the Saturday after the conference. I coped reasonable well with that, but on the Sunday I was desperate for some help. My head seemed to be bursting with all the thoughts going round and round in it. We did see the duty doctor, but he would prescribe nothing but made me an appointment with my own doctor on the Monday. He started me on the same anti-depressant pills that I had had before but warned me that they would have no effect for a fortnight. One thing that they did do was to help me to sleep. How was I going to get through the fortnight until the pills began to work? The doctor had told me to do the barest minimum of housework and rest. His advice was barely necessary, as I had neither the will nor the energy to do it.

I gave up everything at this point. It was a relief not to have to think about anything. I had no interest in food, and meals became very basic. I lost weight, my tendency is to put it on, not lose it. I spent hours lying on the settee staring at the television. Life became too much. Wouldn't I be better off dead? It was another of those occasions – like the grief after Martin died – when getting out of bed in the morning took all my courage and energy. I would put it off for as long as possible.

David wondered what had happened to me, during my previous depression he felt I needed to be occupied and busy and then I would forget myself. To some extent being busy does help; but then in moments when you are not busy you still have to live with yourself. David has a bit of the 'pull yourself together' attitude. This time he could see that that just wouldn't work.

Losing Mum

'Even when I am old and grey, do not forsake me, O God.'
Psalm 71 verse 18

While we were trying to cope with my depression, my sisters, in particular Ann and Rodger were trying to cope with another problem. Mum was now deteriorating rapidly with senile dementia, or what is often called Alzheimer's disease.

I began to notice the deterioration after Dad died. Mum and I had always kept in touch by phone since I had moved away. We used to take it in turns. I found that she rang less and less. I always seemed to make the calls. When I did phone she would have the television on and would get reality mixed up with the TV programme. She would talk to me about what was happening on the screen in front of her and then a member of our own family. As the illness progressed I would ring and she did not even know who I was. Telephoning became pointless so I would ring Ann for news.

The things that worried us particularly were her forgetfulness and out of character behaviour – often manifested in aggression. When Mum could not find things, because Ann was her chief carer, she would get the blame and be accused of taking them to her own home. Usually the things were found hidden away in most peculiar places.

As time no longer meant anything to Mum, we had reports from neighbours that she was up in the night because they saw her light on and heard her bath running. One of the most disturbing things was that she forgot when she had put the gas cooker on. In the end Ann had a special tap fitted so that she could turn the gas off at the back of the cooker. Mum could then only use the cooker when Ann was there to supervise. The other disturbing thing she did was to go 'walkabout' at any time of the day of night, and sometimes with the most peculiar clothes on.

Ann went three times a day to care for Mum and make sure that she was eating properly. Even then she would phone her in between. She cared for Mum like you would a child – but Mum was not a child and she resented this care. I got really worried when I heard how Mum's aggression had led to her attacking Ann with an umbrella. This terrified

Ann as Mum, despite being in her eighties, was not a frail old lady but quite strong. We felt so sad that our Mum who had cared for us so well through the years had changed so much – but we knew it was the illness.

One weekend, when we were staying in Waltham Abbey, Mum went 'walkabout'. Ann had been down to make sure she was up on Sunday morning and had told her we would collect her at 9 a.m. to go to church. Time at this stage of the illness did not mean a lot to Mum. We do not know what went through her mind but when we called to fetch her, she had gone.

We went out searching for her, asking neighbours or anyone else who we thought might have seen her. We finally reported her missing to the police. We did find someone who said they had seen her soon after 8 a.m. but where was she now? We spent the morning searching on foot and by car. What made it worse was that by now it was raining hard.

At about 1 p.m. my nephew, Tim, went out in his car to the police station to take a photograph of his Nan to them. At least then they would know who they were looking for. After delivering the snap, he decided to have one more look for her. He went down by the River Lee to a car park and spotted his Nan just climbing into a car with two strangers. Tim got into his car and followed them. They took Mum to Waltham Abbey and were very kindly trying to find her home. When they finally stopped, Tim jumped out and explained who he was and brought Mum back to Ann's.

When she came in she was cold, wet, exhausted and very distressed. She kept trying to explain what had happened but could not get the words out. As far as we could work out she had gone somewhere to meet us all. Where she had gone we never did find out. We did discover that she had walked to within a few yards of my other sister Joan's home at Enfield because some of her belongings were found there. We worked it out that she must have walked about 6 miles that day.

Ann was at the end of her tether so she contacted the doctor. He arranged for a Psycho-geriatrician to come out and assess Mum. He came at one of her more lucid moments and his report said she was 'delightfully confused'.

We enquired about the possibility of getting her into a home to be looked after, but as we had found with Pop, homes only want old people who can look after themselves.

One home did offer to give her a try and Ann and Rodger took Mum there for a day's trial. Having got her there the matron said, "Let her stay for a day or two so that we can see how she gets on".

It was hopeless; every time she could, Mum was out of the door and going home. They took her handbag away from her to try to discourage her but this only brought out her aggression. She was transferred from there to a mental hospital for assessment.

The hospital was one of the old-fashioned, huge mental asylum-type hospitals (which has since closed). Unfortunately, this turned out to the place where Mum spent her last few months. We did not want her to stay there, it was not the place we would have chosen for her, but none of us could have coped with her at home and she needed full time care and supervision.

Once the initial assessment was over my sisters went every day to see Mum. She deteriorated fast and they were not sure how much she knew them, but Ann usually managed to get through to her. She never smiled now, whereas throughout her life she had been a smiler. Mostly she looked either frightened or blank.

Many of the women in that ward seldom had visitors. Joan and Ann continued to go even though it depressed them to see Mum. They felt guilty leaving her in that dreadful place where she had no dignity and no love.

One day they went in and found Mum badly bruised, very upset and frightened. They never found out exactly what had happened.

As soon as Mum went into hospital she began losing weight and we could not find out how much she was eating. Ann took her biscuits, fruit juice and chocolate as a treat each time she went and fed her with it. In the end Mum stopped taking medicine, wasn't eating and finally stopped drinking, until on November 25th she died. The official cause of death was bronco pneumonia and senile dementia.

We were all with her the day she died, but David and I had to leave to come home about 3 p.m. Both my sisters and brother-in-law Rodger were with her when she died at about 5 p.m. She seemed to be having trouble breathing and then all of a sudden she smiled for the first time in months and died. I wonder who she saw in those last moments to make her smile like that? Was it Dad, Martin or maybe Jesus?

It was such an ignominious end for such a lovely lady but many of her friends and family attended the funeral at the Methodist Church where she had been a member for years. During her illness many of her friends had lost touch with her but they still cared about her and wanted to say goodbye. We had Mum's favourite hymn 'The Lord's my shepherd' sung to the tune 'Crimond' which she had loved for as long as I can remember. She delighted in singing the alto part in her strong voice.

I pray that a cure will soon be found for senile dementia as it is a most degrading and sad illness. People who have it change so much that their characters are not the people you have known and loved for years. You have to remind yourself all the time that what they do and say is attributable to the illness and not really them doing or saying it.

What do I miss about Mum? I'm an orphan now. My biggest connection with my early years is all gone. She was a Christian and a caring person. I miss having her to talk to. If there were ever any news, good or bad, Mum would be the first to tell. I knew she would always be interested. She was another person I turned to for advice, which I seldom took!

CHAPTER TEN

A New Me!

Out into the Sunshine Again

> *'This is the word that came to Jeremiah from the Lord: "Go down to the potter's house, and there I will give you my message." So I went down to the potter's house, and I saw him working at the wheel. But the pot he was shaping from the clay was marred in his hands; so the potter formed it into another pot, shaping it as seemed best to him.'*
> Jeremiah 18 verse 2–4

Mum's illness and death came at a low point in my depression and no doubt added to it. This second bout of depression was so much worse than the first and as it followed so quickly after it, the doctor arranged for me to see a psychiatrist. I was not very thrilled by that thought. I had this stereotyped idea of what a visit to a psychiatrist would be like. You know what I mean, a strange looking man, a couch and all that.

My first visit destroyed that image right away. The psychiatrist was an ordinary looking, gentle, man. We sat opposite each other in a pleasant room and I found myself very quickly at ease with him – we could have been there for a chat over afternoon tea. He soon got me talking about myself and my feelings. I found both sessions I had with him very helpful. It was on his recommendation that I went on to group therapy at Cheadle Royal Hospital. I met first with the psychotherapist, Joan, who also made me feel very at ease, then I joined the group.

I was still unable to drive and the timing of the group meeting, 4 p.m. till 5.30 p.m. on Wednesdays, made it very difficult for anyone to take me – most of my friends had schoolchildren and needed to be at home at that time. Nevertheless, several of them got together and arranged a rota to take me there. David was able to pick me up after work so at least it only had to be one way. I am so grateful for this practical help; they did this for me from October 1989 through until May 1990 when I had regained enough confidence to drive myself.

I was anxious as I approached the room where the psychotherapy group was to be held. The only member I had met before was Joan and there were about eight of us there. The room was always hot and smoky as many of the group members smoked. The hospital is directly under the flight path near to Manchester airport and if you opened a window the planes would drown out any conversation. I felt very strange and wondered what exactly was expected from me in the group. Could talking in a group like this help me anyway? I had talked to Christian friends before, but would I be able to talk as freely in a group of mostly non-Christians. As time went on I found a certain freedom in talking to strangers and non-Christians. They had no preconceptions or false expectations of me, and the way I thought and behaved.

I am quite a shy person, so it took a while for me to actually speak much in the group. I felt that the other people's problems were so much greater than mine and, therefore, their need to talk was also greater than mine.

There were so many problems in that group. The after effects of child sexual abuse, childlessness, attempted suicide, desperate loneliness, the after effects of marriage break ups, the pressure of long term illness of parents and eventually their deaths, lack of love in childhood, rejection by parents, just so much pain.

One helpful thing which was spelled out to me right at the beginning was that feelings are neither right nor wrong they are just feelings. I saw for myself that that was true, feelings come unbidden, the right or wrong bit comes from what we do with those feelings, the actions we take.

When we met, there would usually be one person who came with a burning problem, which was shared in the group. This would trigger things off for other members. Joan would direct us to connect our reactions with painful childhood memories that are often the trigger for our reactions now. She would repeat 'only connect' at frequent intervals. The psychotherapist talks about the 'body memory of the inner child.' I suppose I would call them 'inbred gut reactions' Throughout childhood we are conditioned by what is said and done to us and these affect our reactions and self-images now.

The kinds of things we remember are thing like Mum saying 'if you don't eat all your dinner you won't get any pudding' – even now we feel guilty if we don't clear our plate! Or Dad saying 'You're stupid! You'll never amount to a string of beans!' Or a nickname like 'jumbo' might never allow you to think of yourself as slim even when you are. Those things and worse dog us into our adult lives.

One of the most difficult and painful memories which I had to cope with was Dad's reaction to me when he came back after the war. He had left a baby and came back to a 7 year old. He didn't know how to cope and when I ran to him saying "Daddy, Daddy, Daddy"' back came his response, "How do you know I'm your Daddy?" How could I know, I was just a baby when he left? I ran away to my room and cried myself to sleep.

I can now understand something of my father's reactions and difficulties, but to that 7-year-old child what Dad said was total rejection. I felt this rejection too when I discovered that, being born so soon after my sister, my coming was more of a shock than a joy.

Joan talked about what puts the 'press' into depression and suggested that it was often repressed anger. I found over the months, that through the group I learnt a lot about myself and my inner feelings. As other people shared their problems, it did help to put my own more into perspective. I learnt that there was a lot of repressed anger in me. We were taught to talk or write out our feelings. Writing them down just as they come really does help.

I was angry with God for taking my son from me – I thought I had dealt with this anger but found it was still there. I was angry at Pop for living with us for all those years. I was angry about the insensitive way doctors had treated me, two particular incidents came to mind. The first happened when I was just in labour with Martin and the doctor prodded my tummy and said, "There are too many limbs here, it may be twins". I was carted off to X-ray and told it was not twins. Left to myself I imagined one child with extra limbs. The relief I felt when a normal healthy boy was born you can't imagine. Why didn't that doctor keep her thoughts to herself?

The second was when I had my gall bladder removed. Waking up from the operation I found that I had a drip in my arm and a drain in my side. I thought I must be desperately ill and only found out much later, that this was normal procedure.

At the time of the Gulf War I expressed my anger at Saddam Hussein to the group. Joan suggested that I wrote a letter to Saddam Hussein, not actually to be sent, but to let out my feelings. I found it very helpful and read it out in the group.

Admitting the anger was a start and at that point I felt I had a distinct advantage as a Christian. I could ask forgiveness for my anger and ask for the grace to forgive those who had hurt me and made me angry. I feel the pain from these things from time to time, though it is lessening and the anger is dissipating.

We all suffer rejection from time to time and I still suffer pain when it happens to me, but recognizing that it is opening old wounds makes it that bit easier to cope with.

As I talked or listened in the group I discovered that many of the fears I have are specifically mine. I had always thought that everyone shared them, but each one of us has our own particular set of fears.

One day after I had been to group therapy I gained the realization that I, as a person, was significant, that I had the right to be me. I didn't have to try to be anything or anyone else; I was allowed to be me! As I almost danced along the street I looked at the people I passed and acknowledged their right to be themselves too. Until that day I had spent too long trying to be what I thought other people wanted me to be, God, my parents, my husband, my family, the church. Now I am free and have the right to be me! The key to this realization came when in the depth of my depression I gave up everything. It was at that point that God was able to begin to show me that my true value lay not in what I did but in what and who I **am**.

As I came slowly through this nightmare I see various factors that helped. David was sometimes a great strength at others he was a positive hindrance. It is hard for someone who had never been depressed to understand and cope with depression. He is learning to be a good listener and gives me a reassuring hug whenever I ask him – and even sometimes now even when I don't.

Judy was a great help. She has been through depression herself. On many occasions she was at the end of a phone when I was desperate. She helped me to learn to live; not a day at a time, but an hour at a time, if that was all I could manage to cope with. Looking at a whole day stretching ahead can seem endless when you are depressed. The 'phone calls would often be first thing in the morning and I would say, "I don't know how I'm going to get through the day".

She would reply, "You don't have to. Are you washed and dressed?"

I would often say, "No."

Then she would speak to me like a mother talking to a young child: "Well go and do it now. Once that's done think of the next thing that you need to do."

I have many friends who prayed, visited or lent a listening ear.

I found a set of tapes produced by Rev. Kathleen Bowe, which explain what depression is; they were very helpful.

Prayer inside and outside church was always helpful.

One day that helped a great deal was a 'healing day' spent at Ellel Grange, a Christian Healing Centre near Lancaster. David came with me that day and it was wonderful how God put us with just the right couple. We went in and sat where we pleased and in between sat counsellors on the next row. I went out of the room for a minute and when I came back David was talking to a couple in the next row. They were from New Zealand they, like us, had experienced the death of a son – so we had that in common to start with. Exactly how I was ministered to is a bit hazy but there was a lot of prayer with laying on of hands. My worst fears were dealt with that day and a lot of healing took place.

Through the depression my relationship with God has deepened and improved. I feel a greater trust in Him and look forward to my daily quiet times with Him. The forgiveness that He has enabled has been a key factor in the improvement in that relationship. People tell me that I have changed for the better as a person, I cannot see that for myself, but certainly relationships with many people have improved. It seemed as if I was like the jar in the text at the beginning of this chapter that was smashed and remade into something new and more useful. I hope so.

Again that verse echoes in my mind *'All things work together for good for those who love God.'* As I come to the point of climbing out of the pit into the sunshine again, I can see that God has been at work throughout this time.

God Incidents

'And we know that in all things God works for the good of those who love him, who have been called according to his purposes.' Romans 8 verse 28

I had been attending group psychotherapy for some months and gained much benefit from it. With my faith being an integral part of my life, I had talked in the group about it and how it helped me. I had decided that the time had come to leave but wanted to give them each a leaflet to explain the Christian faith. Then another of those incidents that are bad but which God turned around for good happened. I was asked to write a short leaflet to be handed out at a flower festival we were having at church. We anticipated a lot of visitors over that weekend and we wanted to give them something to make them think about what the church is for. I found myself writing what evolved into a Christian tract. At the last moment, the committee rejected it and this brought back all my feelings of rejection.

The following Wednesday when I went to therapy the leader Joan, looked at me and said, "How are you this week?" She seldom did this, usually leaving the group to get itself started. I was still feeling very hurt about the rejection of my tract, so I told them the whole story. The result was that each member of the group said they wanted to see what I had written to see why it was so bad that it had been rejected. They had given me the perfect opportunity and the next week they each received a copy of the leaflet and wondered what all the fuss had been about.

This and the following incident of healing make me wonder how God can find the time to be so interested in such small things in our lives. With so many millions of people living in the world how can he have time for just me?

About four years previously, after a period of severe indigestion and one or two occasions when I got food stuck in my throat, I had been diagnosed with a hiatus hernia . This had caused me a lot of discomfort and pain until within the last six months the doctor gave me some new treatment, which was so good I forgot I even had a hiatus hernia. Unfortunately, he assured me that it could only be a short-term treatment and the time came for me to come off it. The symptoms returned with full force and the ordinary antacid hardly seemed to touch it at all. I would take some before going to bed then wake in the middle of the night with my stomach seeming to be on fire and take some more. To keep the acid down I tried to prop myself up in bed but got sciatica from sleeping at a strange angle.

One Sunday morning I preached in my own church and in the sermon mentioned the danger of New Age alternative medicines. After the service a lady came to speak to me. She had been ill for several months with a viral infection, which had left her with swollen painful joints.

She said. "My GP has recommended a course of acupuncture. What do you think about that?"

"I'd rather you didn't have acupuncture, I'd rather you asked for prayer or even a course of prayer. At least give God a chance to heal you before you resort to acupuncture."

"I'll think about it", she replied.

That evening another member of our church, Hilary preached and at the end of the service she asked anyone who needed prayer to come forward. The lady I had spoken to in the morning went forward. She was not completely healed straightaway but was so much better.

During the week as I thought about the advice I'd given her I recognized that I needed to take my own advice. I'd had prayer several times but decided to ask again.

Hilary and another friend, Daphne came to pray for me. I didn't feel particularly full of faith, just determined to give God another chance.

They came, and first of all we asked God for forgiveness for our sins. We didn't want any unforgiveness to be a blockage to God's power. Then they prayed and laid hands on me. One prayed and commanded my body to come back into order. As they prayed I felt something happening in the region of the hernia. Afterwards the other shared a picture she had of a light shining on me but being partially blocked by a grey stone. She felt there was something in my childhood that was partially blocking the healing. The only thing I could think of was the rejection, which we talked about and they prayed for.

I was not prepared to say, at that moment, that I had been healed; I knew the biggest test would come when I went to bed that night. On the other hand I knew something had happened to me.

After my evening meal I felt some discomfort so I thought, "I won't be stupid, I'll take some medicine". When it came to bedtime I felt fine so I didn't take any then. I decided I would lay down properly that night, take out the extra pillow I had been using and see how I got on. This I did and slept through until about three a.m. The moment I woke up I knew there was something different – no burning in my stomach!

David is cautious about claiming healing (so am I) and he warned me "Don't go telling everyone you've been healed, you know how you've been disappointed in the past". I agreed with him and only told the two friends who had prayed what had happened. It was only as the healing continued that I began to tell people, I like to give God the glory for what He does. I did have the return of some symptoms during the first three weeks but, as I stood my ground and praised God, they disappeared.

A New Generation

'His mercy extends to those who fear him from generation to generation.' Luke 1 verse 50

Sally phoned one day very excited to say she was pregnant and we were almost as delighted as they were. However, our delight was short lived as she miscarried and had to wait a year or so to become pregnant again. She gave birth to Andrew James in November 1993.

I remember that night so clearly, we knew Sally had gone into labour earlier that day and was going into hospital, but we had no further news for hours. When bedtime came neither David nor I could sleep. At about three in the morning David could contain himself no longer and rang the hospital. That was such an uncharacteristic thing for David to do – if I'd suggested doing it he would probably have discouraged me but he was so anxious and excited that he did it without me saying a word. He got through to the hospital and they said, "We'll just get your son-in-law."

When Simon came to the phone, he was excited and relieved, and said, "We have a son Andrew James born just a few minutes ago."

"Are they alright?" asked David.

"They're fine although the baby's head is a bit bruised and Sally is sore.

He decided to stick his head the wrong way and caused problems. He's very sleepy and Sally's exhausted because of the long labour. I'll speak to you in the morning."

We did get a little sleep that night but couldn't wait till the morning when we hoped to go and see our first grandchild.

Next day we arranged to meet Simon, take him out for lunch and then go on to the hospital. It was such a joy as we entered that hospital ward to see first Sally, exhausted but happy, then dear little Andrew – bruised and battered but beautiful anyway. The love we felt for him was almost overwhelming. Lancaster became a very attractive place from that time on – we did not want to miss a moment of this new child's life.

Simon took a week off from work to look after Sally and Andrew but then I went to stay for a while to help her recover and find her feet. I have such lovely memories of that time, having my first cuddles with Andrew was special. I have a picture etched in my memory of Simon sleeping on the sofa after night duty with his tiny new son sleeping soundly on his chest.

Watching a baby grow and develop is a privilege for parents and grand-parents alike. Andrew has always been far too nosey for his own good. From tiny he has been interested in everything and everyone around him. At times, you knew he was tired but was too interested to go to sleep. He had a fan of soft blond hair that stuck up from the top of his head. It is thicker and coarser now and he has it cut very short to keep it neat but it still sticks up. He is still interested in everything and everyone and goes out to meet them with a smile.

Andrew flourished and Sally got over her tiredness and went back to work, leaving Andrew with a friend, who was a childminder, when Simon was on shift. After about a year she became pregnant again and Eleanor Joy was born in August 1995.

That night is etched on my memory too. I had volunteered to go up as soon as Sally went into labour to look after Andrew, and to allow Simon to be with Sally at the hospital. The call came in the night and I was in the car and on the road to Lancaster within half an hour. David said, "I've never seen you get up and out so quickly!"

I'm usually slow at coming round and getting out. The journey from Knutsford to Lancaster usually takes me an hour in my little Peugeot 205

– there was so little traffic that night that I managed it in 50 minutes. When I arrived they were already in their coats and gently woke Andrew to tell him I was going to stay with him while they went to the hospital to get the new baby.

When I went to the hospital the following day and saw Eleanor Joy laying on the bed her hair was almost black, I gasped and said, "She's the image of Nanny Colla!"

I'm not one for noticing great likenesses in babies, I think it takes time for likenesses to develop, but this time it shouted at me. Nanny Colla was my maternal grandmother.

As with Andrew the love was there. Love is strange it does not divide; it multiplies by the number of people you have to love!

Eleanor as a baby was very different from her brother. She was much more cautious with her smiles and would weigh you up with wide blue eyes before granting you the joy of her smile. Her hair lightened in colour going almost blond in the sunshine. Now her smile is as ready as her brother's and they have become a great part in our lives.

CHAPTER ELEVEN

Retirement

Moving on Again!

'Even when I am old and grey, do not forsake me, O God,
till I declare your power to the next generation, your might to
all who are to come.' Psalm 71 verse 18.

During those early years of our Grandchildren's lives the hour's journey
from Knutsford to Lancaster precluded us from seeing the family too
often and we could not help out with many babysitting duties. One day
when we had to, yet again, say 'no' to a plea for a babysitter David turned
to me and said, "How do you fancy moving nearer Sally and Simon when
I retire?"

"I don't want to move, we're settled here. We've been here 25 years
I'm happy here. I like the church and we have so many friends."

The idea persisted and it did make sense in some ways. We had to
accept that we were getting older and that it would be easier if we were
nearer to them for all our sakes. Some friends had moved when they were
in their seventies but did not have the energy to make new lives for themselves. They did not settle. If we planned to go earlier, we reasoned, we
could choose where we lived and make a new life for ourselves. Then,
even if their work took them to another part of the country, we could
still be content.

As retirement loomed closer we took a holiday in Lancaster using their
house as a base while they were away and spent the time looking around
the area to see where we might want to live. We did not want to live in
Lancaster itself, but the area around is beautiful and close to the Lakes
and Fells of Cumbria.

This move was David's idea but was it also God's idea? By this time we'd
lived in Knutsford for nearly 28 years and it had been difficult settling there

when we first arrived. Did I really want to uproot at 60 and go to another area and start again? As I prayed and pondered the idea I remembered some words God had spoken to me in my quiet time at least 3 years before. He'd said, "Come out from among them". I did not understand what He meant by it but could not forget it. The previous year too our Minister, Dan, had preached at a valedictory service for Pam, who was going off to train to become a Minister, on the subject: "It's time to move on."

Then things began to happen quickly. After our trip to Lancaster we drove back through Garstang; we liked this small town and thought it could be a good place to live. On the way through we noticed a building plot with a board with a builders name and phone number. We rang the builder:

"What are you building on the plot off Lancaster Road in Garstang?"

"There are 8 plots and you can choose your plot and I'll build you whatever you want within reason, only houses though no bungalows."

"When will they be built because we don't want it until the end of 1998?"

"Suits me fine, I'm in no hurry."

So we met him, chose our plot, got in touch with the surveyor who would plan our house for us and began thinking what we wanted.

It must be God's planning I thought; how often do you find a house in a quiet cul-de-sac 3 minutes from the town centre, and a builder who is willing to build what you want, when you want it?

Then I got cold feet, I did not want to move anywhere I wanted to stay where I was and I said to God "But I don't want to move to Garstang!" Back came the reply as quick as a wink: "You didn't want to move to Knutsford." That was quite true, but I knew how much God had blessed me in Knutsford – being baptized with the Holy Spirit within 2 years of arriving there.

Then on 16 January 1998 I opened U.C.B. (United Christian Broadcasters Ltd) 'The Word for Today' notes and began to read. The text at the top was:

'*My God shall supply all your needs.*'

The second paragraph read:

'*Are you thinking about moving? God knows <u>where</u> you'll succeed and He'll direct you if you'll get close enough to Him to listen. In the middle of the*

biggest depression ever to hit the nation, God told Elijah, "Turn thee east-
ward and hide thyself by the brook ... I have commanded the ravens to feed
thee <u>there</u>." (1. Kings l7: 3 —4) The will of God for your life is tied to <u>peo-
ple and places</u>. If God has told you that he wants to bless you <u>there</u> and you
decide to stay <u>here</u> — you'll be disconnected from your source.'

We continued with our planning and chose the design of the house.
Then we hit a snag: David's retirement was put back for a year to
December 1999. This move was not proving to be easy but David said
he would travel to Manchester each day for that final year while I settled
into Garstang.

In July we visited Garstang again and found that our house was already
being built and would be ready much sooner than we expected. The
builder asked us for more money. We went straight back to put the house
on the market and set about finding the cash. On 6 August we had a
letter from our solicitor returning our deposit and saying the house had
been sold to someone else, all our thoughts and plans gone for nothing.
We'd even ordered bathroom and kitchen equipment for the house.
Fortunately, all the tradesmen returned our cash.

What now? We were gutted, should we still move or was God closing
the door to us? Once we'd calmed down we thought about what had
happened with our move to Cheshire, how God had sorted that out for
our good. The reasons for moving were still the same so we decided to
look for another house in Garstang.

Back we went for a week and were generally very disappointed with the
property we saw. We went to look at a house in Larch Grove but
although it was really too big and expensive we decided to put in an offer.
Almost opposite was the house we live in now. It too was up for sale, but
we hesitated to go and see it because it belonged to the surveyor who had
done our planning for the other house. In the end David said, "This is
silly we know that house, we've been in it several times, we like it and
it's a lot cheaper. He didn't have anything to do with the gazumping.
Let's go and see it."

We did, and bought a house that suited us better and was cheaper too!
Though we spent a lot of money on getting it, as we wanted it, during
the first year we were here. We have a south facing back garden, good
neighbours and it is only slightly further from the town.

Divine (or not so divine) Appointments

'Do not forget to entertain strangers for by so doing some
people have entertained angels without knowing it.'
Hebrews 13 verse 2

God moves in mysterious ways to arrange for you to meet people in your life and this time it was my vanity that got me to meet Margaret W.

Like most women I am very conscious of how I look and I love clothes – colourful clothes at that. My friend Daphne and her daughter Marion had been to see a colour consultant and were very impressed with the difference it had made to their colour choices. Wearing colours that suited them made them look so much better and feel more confident.

It was around Christmas time when I decided to treat myself to one of these consultations. My appointment was for 2 p. m and I was apprehensive as I entered the building. I had on my favourite turquoise sweatshirt with matching earrings and Margaret made me feel at ease straightaway by saying "That colour really suits you!"

From then on conversation flowed easily. We talked about our families, our health, our faith or lack of it. In between she tried the colours against my skin and colouring, and made up my face.

As we talked she told me that she was in a battle with cancer and had tried many means including prayer for healing and alternative therapies. She had been brought up a Methodist like me, but did not go to church, although the basics of faith still seemed to be in her. She was interested to hear about my Christian faith and people don't have to ask me twice for a testimony!

My appointment had been for one hour but I was conscious that it was dark and glancing at my watch I saw that it was after 4 p.m. but neither of us wanted to stop talking to the other.

The consultation ended at 5 p. m. As we parted she said, "Thank you for a wonderful afternoon of fellowship. I'd like to give you your colours as a gift!" – thus waiving the rather expensive fee!

~

I have suffered for many years with IBS (Irritable Bowel Syndrome). Many mornings I have diarrhoea with bloating, wind and pain too. There are times when I cannot leave the house until after lunchtime and by then I feel completely drained. I've had prayer many times, various tests, medications of all sorts, and various exclusion diets. Travelling can be a nightmare – wondering when the next 'comfort stop' will be. This kind of anxiety makes the problem worse.

Reaching another low point of despair I decided I would try alternative medicine. Daphne recommended a herbalist who had cured a menopausal problem for her. When I tried to contact her, she had retired, and another name I was given, had moved away. In desperation we tried yellow pages. Thumbing down the list David said, "This one looks hopeful, she or he is a Dr with loads of letters after his/her name. It's in Wilmslow".

We arrived at a large house set in wide grounds and sat apprehensively in the rather ramshackle porch waiting to be summoned for our appointment. When eventually we were called, it was by a frail, elderly lady who showed us into her consulting room where her even more elderly husband sat waiting for us. As she conducted the consultation she turned to her husband for help and advice from time to time. He seemed to me, by his responses, to be in the not so early stages of Alzheimer's disease.

"How can I help you?" she asked.

I proceeded to reel off all the things that were wrong, the operations I'd had etc. in the way you would to a doctor. Appendicitis she knew and also gall bladder, but when I talked about hiatus hernia and duplex kidneys she turned to her husband, who muttered something, more to himself, than to us.

Obviously her doctorate was not in medicine!

We were there for hours and some of the things she said did make some sense to me but then she said, "I believe the food you are eating is blocking your bowel".

I personally thought it was the opposite – but I was just the one suffering with diarrhoea!

Then she asked, "Do you want me to treat you? It will take some months, I will give you some medicine to take – the first bottles will cost £40. You'll need to come back for more".

"What's in the medicine?" I asked.

She mentioned several things that meant nothing to me. I did not know what to do I was desperate, what should I do?

Eventually I agreed and she prepared the bottles of medicine. We paid up and left.

As we drove home panic hit me: she could poison me, I did not know what was in the brew. There was no way I could take that potion! David was not a happy man!

It made me even more aware of how careful you have to be when you go into alternative medicine.

Garstang

. ' "For I know the plans I have for you", declares the Lord, "plans to prosper you and not to harm you, plans to give you hope and a future." ' Jeremiah 29 verse 11

This text was sent to me just after we moved to Garstang and has been an encouragement ever since.

All our worries about the 'frozen north' when we moved to Knutsford, and now we have moved 60 miles further north still, seem rather silly now! I remember a conversation with my elder sister Joan. As we talked I heard a lad's voice in the background, "who are you talking to Nan?" asked Danny. "It's Auntie Doreen, you know, the one that nearly lives in Scotland!" I suggested that might be a slight exaggeration!

We have found, however, that we are in a very beautiful area of the country. We are close to the sea at Blackpool and Morecambe, near the Pennines, the Forest of Bowland and Yorkshire but, most important for David, close to the Lake District where he loves to go fell walking with the Ramblers' Association. Garstang itself is a pleasant market town with sufficient shops to supply our daily needs.

We moved in on 19 December 1998 and some of our neighbours sent us Christmas cards, which was a lovely welcome. The house itself needed a lot of work to make it into the home we wanted.

We did not settle at the first church we attended. Our membership was automatically transferred from Knutsford Methodist Church to Garstang Methodist Church and we carried on our preaching, but we did try the others before we decided where we felt God wanted us to be. Then one day I was in the Methodist Church at a service when I felt deep inside,

"This is your home." Not an easy choice for me, I prefer something livelier, but it does mean I can continue with Local Preaching.

In that first year David left the house early to travel to Manchester daily, while I coped with the workmen. Builders, plumbers, electricians, kitchen planners and fitters came and went and I became 'go between' and 'go for', as I travelled to Preston or Lancaster choosing a kitchen and carpets, wallpaper and curtains.

When I said to David one day, "I'm lonely!", he replied, "Well get out and meet people!" No chance, someone had to look after the workmen and do the running around!

We did gradually get to know people in church and in the Grove. We got talking to Joy and Norman at the end of a service. Joy was a ray of hope for me; she had belonged to a Pentecostal Fellowship before she had moved up from Bristol. She came to be with her daughter who has multiple sclerosis. She had been a widow for some years but then met and married her second husband, Norman. Joy and I go to Scribblers and we encourage each other as Christians.

I was invited to a Women's Bible Study called Tuesday Group that is held fortnightly in the morning at the Free Methodist Church. When I went for the first time, they were doing a study that was built around a story of a woman who had moved miles away from friends and family. It spelled out her loneliness and how an acquaintance had invited her to a Bible study. I felt at home straightaway but rather weepy, it was so like my own situation.

There was another coincidence that morning. We sat in a circle and I could not take my eyes off the lady opposite, she was called Sue. I just knew I had to speak to her. A few weeks before I had preached at a country chapel in Goosnargh and an elderly lady had asked me to pray for her son David. I spoke to Sue afterwards and her husband is the David I had prayed for. Praise the Lord!

I received details of a Creative writing, Stage A course at White Cross Adult College in Lancaster and took my courage in both hands and went along. I enjoyed the course and learnt a lot with an interesting tutor and group of people. I followed this with Stage B the next year. I gained a lot more confidence in my writing and tried writing poetry, plays and monologues, with varying success.

After the Millennium came with hardly a whimper David said, "I'm going to evening classes to learn to play golf".

"I'll come too, I have no wish to become a golf widow!"

We really enjoy it; I wish I had learnt years ago!

We also joined the bowls club – David is very active but I just go for a weekly 'roll up'.

I have joined one energetic group, this is a line dancing class held in the local leisure centre on Monday mornings. It takes brainwork to remember the steps and quick footwork to carry them out. I enjoy the music too. Dancing of any kind is said to be good exercise and good exercise for the brain as well. I hope it will keep dementia at bay! After three years my feet still get in a tangle at times and I forget which step comes next.

We also started a House group and had some good Bible studies with up to ten people present. The prayer times brought wonderful answers. Two I particularly remember praying for were a kidney for a friend's mother and a new knee for my sister-in-law; both were answered much sooner than we dared hope.

After I finished the second creative writing course I joined the Scribblers group at the local arts centre. Being in a group like this spurs you on to write. We read our work out to each other for criticism and encourage each other to enter competitions. We all write very differently.

I received details from Lancaster University of a weekend course for writers in December. I think it was called 'Increase your Writing Power'. My friend Daphne from Knutsford likes to write but doesn't have much time for it so I suggested she and her husband might come and stay with us. The men could entertain themselves while we went off to the university.

We enjoyed the course although we were not too happy with the way the tutor conducted it, but it did get us writing. I wrote the basis of an article about anosmia – having no sense of smell. This is a disability I have had from childhood that has caused me problems and amusing situations too.

In May 1999 Sally and Simon dropped the bombshell that they were thinking of moving to the country. Both their jobs are in Lancaster so it would have to be within easy reach but that could still take them miles away from us. We had always known that this was a possibility but to happen so soon, my heart sank.

They spent the next year looking around the area and put in offers on several houses in different places. Finally, they made an offer on a house in Dolphinholme, which is actually nearer to us than they were before. The house was in a bad state and they lived with us for 5 weeks from the end of April 2000 while they got the house habitable.

By this time we were much more settled and drawn into babysitting for the children and sometimes taking or collecting them from school. If Sally and Simon go out for the evening at the weekend, we have the children to stay overnight and we enjoy having them all to ourselves although by the time they leave we are worn out.

In 2001 I had the growing feeling that I should try to get an alpha course going in our church. I talked about this to the house-group, they were wholeheartedly behind me and said they would help. One thing that spurred me on was when a woman at line dancing asked me, "Do you know anything about the Alpha course?"

"Yes, it's very good, why?"

"My daughter's been to one and she says I ought to go."

"That's interesting, I'm thinking of running one at our church. Shall I let you have the details if we do?"

This was the final spur to me so we put it to the Outreach Group and also the Church Council and it was accepted. I spent a lot of time from then on praying, planning and advertising for it throughout the town.

But still I wondered – was it my idea or God's. Then in my daily readings I read: *'so do the work of an Evangelist, discharge all the duties of your ministry.'* 2 Tim. 4 v 5.

CHAPTER TWELVE

God's Timing

Jubilee Year

> 'Even though I walk through the valley of the shadow of
> death, I will fear no evil, for you are with me; your rod and
> your staff they comfort me.' Psalm 23 verse 4

We had worked hard advertising and praying for the Alpha Course. Our house group were my backing team; I was very nervous it was 'my baby'. We started on Wednesday 23 January with 7 people and lots of helpers. There were eleven people booked on the course and all but one turned up to later meetings.

I found that as problems arose God dealt with them in wonderful ways as the next paragraph illustrates.

A very important part of Alpha is the weekend – or day – away in the middle of the course when the work of the Holy Spirit is considered. We set the date in the original schedule but as the weeks went on, this one and that, said they could not come on that day. I was very disappointed and at first considered changing the date. Other leaders suggested leaving it as it was, as the date had been known as part of the whole course right from the beginning, so that is what we did. Gradually over the weeks all but one said they had rearranged their appointments and only one woman missed it. I had a session with her on her own so that she did not miss the teaching.

It was an excellent day. Some people became Christians for the first time and others were filled with the Holy Spirit and spoke in tongues – others were prayed with for healing. One man was healed of back pain.

Later in the Alpha course there is a session about healing and after the video we allowed the Holy Spirit to move among us giving words of knowledge about peoples need for healing or stirring individuals to ask.

It was a time of stepping out in faith and we prayed with several people.

At the end of the Alpha course we had a celebration supper. All the participants were invited together with spouses and anyone from the church who wanted to come. We had just two people from the church and one of them was the wife of a helper. We were very disappointed with the lack of support from the church in general throughout the whole project. Nevertheless God blessed participants and helpers greatly. We all grew in our faith.

~

Since the university writing course in December I had been working on my article on anosmia (lack of sense of smell) and had tried to place it. I'd polished it, refined it, made it more like an item to read and sent it off to the Home Truths programme on BBC Radio 4. They were interested and John Peel was going to interview me soon to include the subject in the programme.

~

It was in May 2002 that I began to have pain in my left breast. I prodded and poked but could not feel a lump, as such, but it did not feel the same as the other one, so I 'phoned to get an appointment with one of the lady doctors. The doctor I really wanted to see is popular and it is always difficult to get her, so I rang expecting to wait a fortnight but was told there was a cancellation that morning at 10 a.m. Did God have a hand in this?

She examined me thoroughly.

"Don't panic," she said (so I did!) "I'll send you to the breast clinic in Lancaster to have it checked out. I expect it's just the HRT you're on."

I received the appointment very quickly but it was a fortnight hence so we were able to have our week's holiday in the Isle of Man.

The Tuesday after found us at Lancaster Royal Infirmary. We had been warned that it could be a long appointment and we were there for hours. The Consultant examined me and like my GP thought the problem could be the affects of the HRT but suggested a mammogram, then we waited for the results.

It showed something unusual, so I had to wait again until they took 6 biopsies. This involved the breast being clamped into the mammogram machine and the biopsies were 'fired' into the breast. The doctor who did them gave me a local anaesthetic but did not wait for it to work. I yelled and came out of there shaking like a jelly, even after a cup of tea. All this time David sat anxiously in the waiting room. We were then allowed to go, but told to come back in a fortnight for the results. It would have been just a week, but the following Tuesday was the extra bank holiday for the Jubilee (for which we had a street party, but it passed for me, in a blur).

The following day found me on my way to Lancaster again, this time to the BBC studio at the University where I was to be interviewed over the airwaves by John Peel about anosmia. I was very nervous. It is a good job that I am not claustrophobic as the studio is a tiny soundproof room with no windows. It seemed that I sat there for ages until the producer spoke from London, and then he put John Peel on. Once the interview started I enjoyed it and found him very easy to talk to. The item was broadcast on the following Saturday, and I was pleased with the way it came across.

~

At last, June 11 came, so it was back to the Breast Clinic for the results. The Consultant examined me and said they had found something so I immediately asked, "What?"

"It's cancer," he said, "But I didn't intend to tell you that until you were dressed and sitting comfortably in the other room. Get dressed and come through and we'll talk about it then."

It seemed just as though I had been punched, I was stunned, horrified, and yet it was as though he had told someone else – it's always someone else who has cancer isn't it? How bad is it? Am I going to die? What happens now? There were so many questions chasing each other through my shocked mind.

We were soon in the other room with my assigned breast care nurse holding my hand.

"What happens now? How bad is it?" I asked.

The consultant said, "You have two options, you could have a lumpectomy, just taking away the lump and some lymph nodes from under your arm to make sure the cancer hasn't spread into the lymphatic system. If you had this you would definitely need radiotherapy and maybe chemotherapy too."

"What's the other option?"

"A full mastectomy, with some lymph glands taken from under your arm. You might need chemotherapy or radiotherapy or both afterwards. You might just need drug treatment. It depends what we find when we operate.

"I don't know," I almost shouted, "just get it out of me!"

Then he said, "If you have a lumpectomy and I find further cancer I would have to do a second operation, a full mastectomy."

"Supposing I gave you permission to carry on and do a mastectomy if you find further cancer, could you do that?"

"No," he said, "You have to decide. If you make your decision, you could have the operation on Thursday. I'll leave you with the breast care nurse to consider the options and I'll speak to you later."

The nurse was very helpful answering our questions. She showed me what a breast prosthesis looked like – I thought it looked awful and felt even worse. She gave us leaflets about the operations and treatments. She is still my contact point with the hospital. I decided then to have the full mastectomy – at 64 I reckoned I did not really need my breast any more, I was not likely to have another child! I did not want further treatment or another operation if I could avoid it.

When we saw the doctor later he said, "I think you need some more time to think about your decision. I'll book you into hospital next Wednesday for the operation on Thursday."

Wednesday 19 June came and I had to ring the hospital at 10.30 a.m. to check if there was a bed for me. There wasn't but they promised to ring when one became free. Waiting again, this time for the phone to ring.

I came off the phone in floods of tears. This whole episode seems to have been one of waiting. The week since I was told I had cancer has not been the worst week of my life, no, the week we watched our son die after an accident takes that accolade, but the shock of the diagnosis, the fear of cancer, together with the grief I feel for the loss of my breast, makes it a close second.

What follows are extracts from a notebook I kept at the time.

I did get a bed and was assigned a nurse who seemed very nice. The trouble was she went off duty that day and I never saw her again!

I was glad David stayed with me all day, and that, because of the delay, we had had a main meal at home as tea was not very appetizing. The dessert was a chocolate blancmange that must have been frozen and had separated into water and sludge.

That evening I had blood tests and a chest X-ray. I just wanted the whole thing to be over and yet at the same time I dreaded it, it was awful. Back in the ward after the X ray I had a Horlicks at 11 p.m. but could not sleep. I had a sleeping pill and slept fitfully until 3 a.m. the patient next to me was receiving constant attention. I had a hot drink and slept on till about 5.30 a. m when the staff started moving around again.

That night was awful, struggling with thoughts, feelings and fears. At one time in the night I gave my breast back to God and thanked him for the use of it for feeding my children and just being a woman, then I cried again. Then there were the questions, would David still love me after the operation? Would I still feel like a woman with just one breast? Would I even survive breast cancer? How would I cope after the operation I usually get sick after an anaesthetic? How would I cope with the prosthesis? Where are you God?

The morning did come, but I felt like a fish out of water. Not knowing the hospital routine made things difficult and the nurses do not tell you much, you have to find out for yourself.

A breast care volunteer came in and put the fear of God into me.

I asked, "What do I need to know about lymph oedema?"

"You'll have to make sure you don't cut or prick your left hand or arm, you mustn't have injections, blood tests or blood pressure taken on that arm either – they could all start it off"

I'm on a steep learning curve. I can't take it all in. All this has happened since Tuesday I can't cope with it. Information overload.

The nurses made up my bed and when I looked there were thick black hairs all over the sheets. I told the nurses and they changed them. Would they like to have someone else's hairs all over their bed sheets?

I talked to one or two fellow patients.

The operation is over and I'm still alive. David and Sally came to visit. I don't remember anything about their visit. The pain at the back of my arm is excruciating at times – like I've thumped my funny bone – only it isn't funny. Felt sick after anaesthetic. I have two drains in me but this time the doctor had warned me.

Saturday the family came, Andy and Ellie were lovely so concerned and gentle.

I wanted to know what the left hand side of my chest looked like now – and yet I did not. I saw it when I was taken for a bath and there was a mirror on the wall. I could not see it properly because of the dressing but I did not like what I saw. It was months before I could bring myself to touch it.

It's Sunday and I'm waiting for a wash. A lady came in and gave me communion and prayed for healing. It was a lovely oasis.

Some of the nurses are very nice, others couldn't care less, one threw a sheet and it hit my drain bottle and hurt – no apology. I had to supply my own carrier bag to carry the drain bottle around. Life in hospital is chaotic, the nurses are so different, some give care and others just work around you

As soon as I was able, a nice young woman, a physiotherapist, came and showed me some exercises to do. These included walking my hand up the wall. I told the other patients I had had enough and was trying to get out! They called them my 'aerobics'

The woman opposite has got diverticulitis. I know about that, the only thing you can do is learn to manage it. There is no magic wand to take it away. Her son keeps declaring loudly that he wants something to be done!

Another woman, who is 86, sits opposite me looking very fierce, but she can hardly see at all. She has pain in her leg, which is cancerous. To save her life the surgeon wants to amputate the foot. She says no! I have been praying for her ever since I knew. I had the opportunity to talk to her last night.

She said, "I'm not religious, I don't know about God, nobody's told me." I offered to pray for her but she refused.

I told her, "you may not believe in God but he believes in you".

I talked to a woman from Liverpool – now living in Blackpool. She kept going out of the ward to smoke, she's panicking about a mastectomy today, Wednesday. I prayed for her but she was too spooked to expect anything. This was her second operation – she'd already had a lumpectomy.

I went home from hospital on 26th June. David has been re-organising my kitchen – Lord help!

I'm so tired and sore, it is nice, but scary to be home – there's no one to ask about problems although I can ring the breast care nurse any time in office hours.

David is doing everything and coping very well. Even cooking!

He decided he wanted to make a roast dinner on the Sunday after I came home; I had to show him what to do. The element in the oven broke and blew a fuse. We had to finish cooking the joint and vegetables in the microwave and top oven! We were weeks without it.

I am back in waiting mode; we will know the results of the tests on the cancer removed, on Tuesday 2nd July.

At last 2 July we went to the hospital for the results. I had fluid drained off from the wound. The consultant said, "When we operated we found a second cancer".

I am so glad I chose the mastectomy. The lymph nodes were clean so the only treatment was to be Tamoxifen. This treatment was to be confirmed after consultation with the oncologist.

I found out two things nearly a year later, that I had stage 1 cancer and that one of my nerves had been sacrificed in the operation, which is why there was so much pain in my elbow.

Saturday 6 July I was worried about fluid build up but didn't know whom to contact about it. It took an hour and 4 phone calls to eventually find out that I should contact ward 33, where I had had the operation. We went to Lancaster but very little fluid was drawn off.

On Tuesday 9th I went back to the breast clinic and had more fluid drained. It was confirmed that I would need no further treatment but Tamoxifen.

When I found out I had breast cancer I knew of another younger woman at church who had the operation a couple of years before. She contacted me by phone and came round to talk to me about it. She was a great help and at the end of the phone when I needed her. My next-door neighbour helped too as she'd had it some years ago.

When I knew I had to have an operation I had been anxious, as we had planned a holiday with the family in Jersey in August. When I told the doctor he said, "You should be fine to go then, in fact it would do you the world of good!"

This holiday became the thing I worked towards. I remember Sally saying to me "We'll get you there even if I have to carry you on to the aeroplane!"

I got there and enjoyed the rest. It was the pain in my arm that was so debilitating and it was at its height 4–6 weeks after the operation. The holiday was one milestone towards recovery.

The second was starting back at line dancing on 19 August – I took it very gently!

I was still getting a lot of pain and my shoulder was stiff, so the doctor recommended Physiotherapy at LRI. I went for months. It helped a lot.

On 14 September I did a lot of pruning in the garden and got a thorn in my wedding ring finger. I was very anxious after having the mastectomy and the worry of getting lymph oedema. In church on 15th the preacher that day read from Ezekiel chapter 2, verse 6 stood out for me. "Do not be afraid, though briars and thorns are all around you and you live among scorpions." Praise the Lord.

One word of warning I would like to give you: I went to the doctor when I felt pain in the breast, the doctors told me that pain is very unusual in the early stages of cancer so please do not wait for pain, if you feel any lumps at all, see your doctor straightaway.

Appointment in Vienna

'But I trust in you, O Lord; I say, "You are my God." My times are in your hands.' Psalm 31 verses 14 & 15a

2002 had not been a good year. I found it very hard coming to terms with what had happened to me, I knew with my head that 'All things work together for good for those who love God'. I also knew with my head that 'my times are in his hands.' Knowing with my head is one thing but feeling it and knowing in my heart are another, I struggled because I did not <u>feel</u> God near me although I <u>knew</u> he was by how I was cared for. Facing cancer and the possibility of death concentrates the mind on what is important and spurs you on to do things while you have the time and strength.

2003 was to be a mixture of joys and sorrows too. In February I saw an advertisement for a holiday cruise down the Danube and suggested to David that I'd like to do that. We decided to treat ourselves and go.

It was the amazing coincidence of timing, which happened on this holiday, which convinced me that 'my times are in his hands!' I'll tell you the story and you can judge for yourselves.

It was 7.30 p.m. on Saturday 25 June, at last we were standing in reception on our cruise ship MS *Viking Europe* moored in Vienna, that was to take us down the Danube to Constanta.

We booked in and asked, "When is dinner served?"

"It's being served now."

"We'll just go to our cabin and wash and go in", we replied.

"You'd better go now or dinner will be over! We'll take your luggage to your cabin."

So away we hurried and were shown to the only two empty seats right at the end of the dining room. We were the last passengers to arrive.

This was not the way I had wanted to make my entrance on this cruise – we'd heard about the etiquette on cruises and one thing that you did not do, was to go in comfortable trousers and unwashed into dinner!

Our problems compounded when we found ourselves sitting with a couple from Los Angeles, Emil a man of 83, Bulgarian by birth, and his wife Zita, 74, French by birth but both speaking in broken American. It would have been hard enough to understand American but with Bulgarian and French accents as well we had to listen very intently in between the five courses. It was made worse for David who was sitting next to Emil who used expressive hand gestures.

However, from the moment we met we got on well and they made it clear that they liked to sit with the same people for meals if at all possible. No one had set tables, but we did sit with them at most meals. We had a lot of laughs together and David called Emil 'Uncle Bulgaria'. We tried to explain about this name coming from a children's cartoon programme called The Wombles but I don't think he ever understood.

Over the next few days we gradually learnt more about each other and we felt privileged to be sharing this trip with them. They had each made a success of their lives in America he had started out as a 'buzz boy' (I hope I've used the right expression) in a hotel and worked his way up to management. She had been a fashion designer who oversaw Mexican seamstresses speaking only in Spanish. Their knowledge of other languages made me feel lazy with my schoolgirl French and German.

She was always elegantly turned out and being French took a great interest in the food we were served. He was remarkably vigorous for his age and took a great interest in good-looking women, food and politics.

Emil had left his home 50 years ago when the Communists had taken over Bulgaria. He was an army officer and had been imprisoned. He was released but knew that he would be imprisoned again because of his political views.

He made arrangements and set off with his sister-in-law to leave the country. The only option they had was to escape over the mountains to Greece – where they knew they would not be very welcome, as the Greeks and Bulgarians were not the best of friends.

Their route took them over mountains where there were few tracks and only a compass bearing as their guide. They were nearly discovered by the Communists one night but after ten days they arrived at the Greek border. Here they were interrogated and imprisoned. After some time and several refugee camps, other countries became willing to accept Bulgarian refugees; they needed welders and Emil could weld. This was how Emil found himself shipped to Brazil.

It was in Brazil that Emil and Zita met. We never discovered how Zita came to be living in Brazil. They met at a party where neither of them had wanted to go but where persuaded to go by friends. Their romance began in stumbling Portuguese, as neither could speak the other's language, but each of them knew a little Portuguese.

Day by day we learnt more about this amazing couple. Emil's father had been a Congregational Pastor in Bulgaria, which opened the door for us sharing something of our faith. Zita is a Catholic who does not practice her faith but prays. Emil is not a believer but respects those who are. Considering his expressed unbelief he still raised questions about faith that either David or I found, with the Holy Spirit's help, we were able to answer.

One question he asked was "Why didn't the Jews accept Jesus as their Messiah?"

I found myself answering this one by suggesting that it was because the

Messiah they expected was the one portrayed in some of the prophecies in the Old Testament of the conquering war like leader and king, whereas Jesus came as the suffering servant, which they had not considered. It seemed to satisfy him.

The two subjects that are not to be discussed over dinner – religion and politics, were often the very topics that we discussed!

It became clear that the main reason for them coming on this cruise was so that Emil could meet up with his nephew at Vidin – one port in Bulgaria at which we were due to dock. His brothers are both dead and he had never met his nephew, so he was very excited.

We were due to dock in Vidin on Saturday 5 July but due to unforeseen delays we were not now going to dock there until Sunday 6th July. Emil was frantic, as by the time he knew this, he suspected that his nephew and his wife would have already been on their way from Sofia. For about a day and a half he wandered morosely around the ship and did not eat all his meals. Once in Bulgaria he stared out at the banks of the river drinking it all in.

With help from the tour manager, Elizabeth, who knew of his predicament, he finally contacted his nephew by radiotelephone and the meeting time was changed.

At midday on that Sunday 6 July we sailed into Vidin. We were at lunch as we arrived but Emil could not contain himself, left his lunch and went on deck to see his Nephew for the first time. After 50 years he could live without lunch!

Waving from the quay was his nephew, his wife and their son. After lunch we went on deck to rejoice with him and wave to them too. Eventually, customs was satisfied and he was allowed to land while we went with Zita on an excursion to Baba Vida fortress and Belogradshick. Zita reckoned that he needed this time alone with his family after all those years. Later Zita joined them and we saw them on the quay taking photographs.

Once back on board, with the ship preparing to leave Vidin, Emil had a grin on his face as wide as the proverbial Cheshire cat and we celebrated with a bottle of wine at dinner.

Since the fall of Communism in Bulgaria the country is very poor. The people struggle to bring a workable structure back into society. Their way of life before Communism was a simple one with many people owning and working their own land. With Communism the land was owned by large co-operatives and everyone was employed. 5 per cent of Bulgarians are leaving each year. As if to validate that, when we were in Veliko Tarnovo a young woman came up to me in the street – I was wearing my tour badge and we had put a Union flag in the corner – She asked me "Are you from England?"

I said, "Yes."

"Can I ask you what England is like?"

"Of course."

The first question she asked was about the weather "Is it always raining or foggy?"

"No, but we do get quite a lot of rain."

"It is my dream to go to England"

"The streets aren't paved with gold, we have our problems there too," I said. I did not want to shatter her dreams but I wondered where her information about Britain had come from.

We learnt a bit more about the poverty there is in Bulgaria from what Emil said about his nephew. They had no car of their own and had borrowed one. They had a tyre blow out on their trip to Vidin. The car was old and all the tyres were second hand but for their return trip they now had no spare. The irony is that there is a massive tyre factory in Bulgaria, which under communism employed 2,500 people. The tyres were sold to Russia. Now all the tyres the Bulgarians use are imported second hand ones and only 300 people work at the factory, they cannot afford to buy the tyres that are produced there.

Emil's nephew is a Congregational pastor and gave him an English/Bulgarian New Testament, which opened up our talks about faith again. I suspect his nephew had been praying for him and that is why Emil was so full of questions.

After dinner they shared some special bread that his niece-in-law had baked and brought specially for them, with us, it was partly sweet, partly savoury – a bit like croissant – light and different.

Emil and Zita have invited their great nephew to stay in Los Angeles for a holiday and Emil hopes to go back to Bulgaria for a holiday.

When it came time to dock again in Vienna at the end of the cruise,

I wanted to give them something as a memento of our time together and perhaps to encourage their exploration of faith so I gave them Every Day with Jesus for May–June which is about the promise of the Holy Spirit. They have both said they will read it. We have exchanged addresses and feel we have friends in LA.

Cliff

'We have an anchor that keeps the soul steadfast and sure while the billows roll; Fastened to the rock, which cannot move, Grounded firm and deep in the Saviour's love!' (From the hymn 'We have an anchor' by Priscilla Owens)

In April of 2003 we heard from Joan Blanks that David's brother Cliff was in hospital. He had woken one morning and could not get his words out and his legs were unsteady. A brain scan was done revealing what appeared to be a stroke. David went down to see him. Then we heard that he had been sent home to recover. A speech therapist went in each week to help him get back his speech. We spoke to him on the phone but conversations were very strange until, in the end, we just spoke to Joan to ask how he was.

The doctors had expected him to improve but far from this there seemed to be a steady deterioration. We knew before we went on holiday that he had got considerably worse and we promised to keep in touch by phone.

We arrived home to find a message on our answerphone to say that Cliff was back in hospital. He had deteriorated so much that he was sleeping much of the time and had lost control of his bodily functions, which was not what the doctors or Joan had expected. In the end Joan phoned her GP and he told her to call an ambulance. Once back in hospital they repeated the brain scan and there were now two tumours visible and growing fast. Before we could get to see him and within a fortnight of our return home Cliff was dead.

This was an awful shock and after the wonderful illustration of God's timing on our holiday we have to accept that Cliff's death was God's timing too. Shock, grief and bewilderment followed his death. How could there have been no sign of the tumours on the first scan? The doctors were as mystified as we were. His end was undignified and very distressing for all who saw him.

The funeral was an amazing affair. They decided to have the committal at the Crematorium first, followed by a Thanksgiving Service at his home church. He had lived in Chingford all his life. The crematorium chapel was full – it is the only time I have seen people standing packed at the back. There was a guard of honour formed by the bowling club. He was a keen bowler and had won trophies and been captain of the club.

Back at New Road Methodist Church the Thanksgiving Service was held and this too was packed. Cliff had been Leader of the Life Boys and also Boy's Brigade Captain and moving tributes were paid to him from the Church, the Boy's Brigade and then his eldest grandson Matthew (16) spoke. You could have heard a pin drop and there was not a dry eye in the church.

Afterwards refreshments were served in the Church Hall and a collection made for The National Children's Home. The dignity and grace with which Joan conducted herself through all this, amazed us all.

Cliff was eight years older than David and when David was born Cliff thought he was wonderful until he realised that he could not play football! People said that the brothers looked alike and they were alike in their straight talking, sense of humour and teasing, but they were different in other ways. For Cliff, work was a means to an end, he needed the money to keep himself and his family but he was more interested in outside work activities like the Boys Brigade and other church things. Retirement meant that he had the freedom to do the things he wanted all the time. Gardening took over, and then bowling almost became an obsession. On the other hand David was more ambitious and worked hard both at work and in the Church.

We have lived miles apart for many years but there was always a good relationship between us. We will miss him and his teasing!

CHAPTER THIRTEEN

God can be real for you too!

From Bicycle to BMW!

*'But you will receive power when the Holy Spirit come on
you; and you will be my witnesses in Jerusalem, and in all
Judea and Samaria, and to the ends of the earth.'*
Acts 1 verse 8

In June it will be two years since the cancer operation and I have just
received the 'all clear' for another 6 months. I do not know how many
days, weeks, months or years I have left to spend in this world, but none
of us know that. I have told you about my life, it has been rather like a
roller coaster with ups and downs and several plateaux. What I hope I
have shown you through my varied experience, is that God has been with
me all the way through. Not that I have always felt him there – but feelings are not always a very good guide. At times you know that I did not
cope very well with life but I often wondered how people who do not
believe in God could cope at all.

People will say, as they look at the large things in the world, the mountains, the oceans, the sun, the sky and the stars that this points to a
creator God. That is true, but the things that amaze me more are the
small things, for instance the intricacies of our bodies and how the different small parts work together to make our life possible. Or I look at
the parts of a tiny flower or an insect – these speak more to me of a
creator. Jesus says, *"Are not two sparrows sold for a penny? Yet not one of
them will fall to the ground apart from the will of your Father. And even
the very hairs of your head are all numbered."* Matthew 10 verses 29 & 30.
My husband jokes about this last one and says God has an easier job with
him; as he is bald!

The things I have written about in this book have been mostly the big things that have happened, but day-by-day I experience God's love in the small things too. For example, when I received the all clear at the Breast clinic I rang my friend who had breast cancer about 4 years ago, to tell her my good news, when I got through she was really unwell. She'd had a really bad reaction to an antibiotic so I was able to commiserate with her and pray for her before I told her my good news – which cheered her up.

On the same day I went into a shop where I do not usually shop and found myself standing next to a woman who knew me through my preaching, again we encouraged one another, then, as I went back to the car, I met another woman who had taken part in our Alpha course and we encouraged one another. Three small incidents where I felt God had taken a hand.

Joy called today and she shared how she had appointments for 2 men to come and look at her kitchen, she was anxious because there was not much time between the appointments. She prayed about it and one man came five minutes early and the other half an hour late giving them the time they needed! He does not just do these things for me.

How can God care so much for us that he sets up these little surprises for us?

I think of my daughter, as it gets near to Christmas, usually Andrew and Eleanor know what they want for Christmas, but as well as the big present, Sally always prepares a stocking for them and has great delight in finding and hiding small things that she knows they will enjoy. She does it because she loves them and wants to show that love. God is just the same.

Several times I have said that I did not feel God near me when I was in hard places, but I knew he was by what he did in my life. These are the kind of things I mean the small coincidences of timing, being in the right place at the right time, like when we were on holiday in Israel we met a minister we knew at Tel Aviv airport. People who are not Christians would dismiss these as coincidences, but the more I pray the more the coincidences keep happening!

If you do not know Jesus as your Saviour and friend you might like to consider the tract I wrote for the flower festival, it is set out below:

'Flowers – with Love!'

You have come into this Church today to see and appreciate the beauty of the flowers. Flowers are so often given as a gift of love, red roses to a sweetheart, a bouquet on the birth of a child, flowers at an anniversary or as a thank you. Even at funerals flowers are given to show love; these flowers are a gift given in love by God to each and every one of us.

What is God's love like? May I ask you to think of your greatest experience of love, it may be the love of a mother, father, husband, wife, or it may be your own love for your child? Now think of multiplying that 100 times (or more!) and that is how much God loves you! (Warts and all, black and white, male and female, young and old.)

God loves each one of us like that and wants to enjoy a loving relationship with us, that was what we were created for – but there is a problem, God has done nothing to spoil that relationship but we did. We sinned – we turned our backs on God and decided to live our lives in our own way without reference to him. It's just the same with human relationships, sin spoils them too, anger, jealousy, lust, selfishness etc. In human relationships it is usually six of one and half a dozen of the other, but not in our relationship with God. God has done nothing to spoil our relationship with him, – but we have.

But now, here is the good news God did something about it. He took the initiative and sent Jesus his son to live amongst us, to die on the cross and be raised to life again. An innocent man took the punishment for our sin, so that we might be reconciled to God.

What is our part? We have to come in repentance – that is acknowledging our sins and being sorry for them and also wanting to start again. Then we can accept forgiveness and enter into a new life in fellowship with God. Jesus calls this being 'born again'. Once we enter into that relationship we will find a new purpose and fulfilment in life – in the Bible it is called abundant life – it is not just pie in the sky when you die!

It has been said that from the time of our birth we have a God shaped vacuum inside, we try to fill it with so many things, material success, marriage, food, alcohol, smoking, sex, but nothing except God can fill it.'

For this message in a nutshell turn to John chapter 3 v 16. '*For God so loved the world that he gave his one and only son that whoever believes in him shall not perish but have eternal live. For God did not send his son into the world to condemn the world, but to save the world through him.*'

God through sending Jesus into the world and allowing him to die on the cross deals with our past – each one of us has a past that is good in parts and bad in parts – some parts we rejoice over, others we are ashamed of, God can deal with both so that we might become his friends.

Jesus knows you through and through – the best and the worst

– and yet he loves you and wants to be your friend.

Jesus wants to be there for you today, tomorrow and for eternity. When you put yourself into his hands they are safe, loving hands. That doesn't mean there won't be difficulties but he will see you through them. '*"For I know the plans I have for you," declares the Lord, "plans to prosper you and not to harm you, plans to give you hope and a future. Then you will call upon me and come and pray to me, and I will listen to you."* 'Jeremiah 29 v 11–12.

If you would like to know that friendship then you could pray the following prayer:

'*Lord Jesus I invite you into my life. I believe you died for me and that your death on the cross pays for my sins and provides me with the gift of eternal life. By faith I receive that gift and I acknowledge you as my Lord and Saviour. Please baptize me with the Holy Spirit so that I may have the power to live a new life. Amen.*'

Perhaps you feel you would like to have Jesus as a friend but you haven't got the 'faith'. Let me explain what faith is, in Matthew 14 v 22 – 33 is the story of Jesus walking on the water. The story starts as Jesus sends the disciples on ahead of him over the lake while he goes up on the mountain to pray. Later in the night when the disciples were well on their way a wind came up and Jesus set out to walk to them across the

Martin

Why did you leave us twenty years ago
Just sixteen years and so much promise.
We love you dearly but we had to let you go
Your injuries so drastic they left us speechless.
Time is said to be the healer
But still the pain, it lingers
If only we could once more feel a
Touch of your long slender fingers
Upon our cheek or hand or something,
Or hear your voice say "little Mum"
Or "Dad" or just "hello", better much than nothing.
To hear that now we'd be struck dumb.
But still we think how death the cheat
Left us with memories bittersweet.

Martin

Why did you leave us twenty years ago
Just sixteen years and so much promise.
We love you dearly but we had to let you go
Your injuries so drastic they left us speechless.
Time is said to be the healer
But still the pain, it lingers
If only once more feel a
Touch of your long slender fingers
Upon our cheek or hand or something,
Or hear your voice say "little Mum"
Or "Dad" or just "hello", much better thn nothing.
To hear that now we'd be struck dumb.
But still think how death we cheat
Left us with memories bittersweet.

waves, they were terrified –, they thought he was a ghost! Jesus reassures them, then Peter, always the impetuous one, says: *"Lord, if it's you tell me to come to you on the water."*

"Come," he said.

Then Peter got down out of the boat, walked on the water and came towards Jesus.' Before Peter stepped out on to the water he believed it was possible to walk on the water to Jesus but stepping out of the boat was Peter's faith in action. Believing happens in your mind, faith is acting on that belief. Faith could, for you, be demonstrated in praying that prayer.

Perhaps you prayed that prayer and you had a wonderful feeling of peace. Or perhaps you prayed it and had no feelings at all – and you began to doubt.

That is just like Peter, having begun to walk on the water he notices the wind and begins to sink – he doubts what has just happened to him.

Don't doubt what you have done; tell someone about it, your pastor, vicar, minister, priest or a friend who is a Christian. You may have questions, so look for an Alpha course being held in your area and go along. It will help you to understand what you have done.

Perhaps you are someone like me who has lived as a Christian for years without being baptized with the Holy Spirit. We need His power to change us into people who are like Jesus in character and actions. Before Pentecost the disciples hid away, afterwards they went out into the streets praising God, witnessing to his glory and healing the sick – they just could not help themselves. This was my experience. To give you an analogy, for those 23 years of trying to be a Christian in my own strength, it was like pedalling hard on a bicycle and getting nowhere. Once I was baptized in the Holy Spirit it was like being driven in a powerful BMW. Take a leaf out of my book get down on your knees and pray for the baptism in the Holy Spirit then take your seat in the BMW, God needs you and you need Him.

God, who loves you with an everlasting love, bless you all.

Nanny Colla

She sits in the armchair in the corner,
neat bun upon her head,
three pairs of glasses on her nose,
each pair of them bought from a jumble sale
Not one prescribed for her,
Reading, now her greatest pleasure,
Poor sight her toughest enemy.

She struggles up to fullest height
Now almost as wide as she is tall,
She hesitates as, with a tremble
the Parkinsons curbs her steps

Poor sight she might have but her nostrils twitch,
as the odour of curry wafts from the kitchen.
She staggers along with trembling gait
to impart the wisdom she has gained in
India, on how to make that dish to true perfection.

Mum sees her coming with a sigh
She's made it very often and knows,
that although she makes it very well
It won't be to Nan's perfection

I come into the kitchen at the point
when voices start to rise.
I slip away and hope that they
won't come to blows.

The meal when served tastes good to me, but
Nan and Mum eat each mouthful in distant, stony silence.

Line Dancing

At crack of dawn
On Monday morn
I mosey down the leisure centre,
Pay my fee and swiftly enter.
Inside the doors
On polished floors
I engage my brain and then my feet
To lively music with a beat.
One step forward and two steps back
I should by now have got the knack!
Grapevine left then shimmy, shimmy!
Watch out! Nearly trampled Jimmy!
The next one's set to Irish music
Just can't move my feet that quick!
The tutor looks at me askance,
But I'm not part of River Dance!
We'll have a break now she declares
We drink and slump down in our chairs.
We'll learn a new one it's quite easy.
Tutor says, all bright and breezy.
We slowly rise and take our place
In lines, where we can find a space.
Forward with the left, kick ball step,
Shuffle back and quarter left,
Full turn over your right shoulder,
Find I'm getting ever bolder.
We've practised, now the music's on
My inhibitions they have gone.
Line dancing takes such concentration
That all my stress goes on vacation!